Destiny Beyond Abandonment

By
Roger Ray

Paperback

ISBN: 978-1-966606-26-0

Hardcover

ISBN: 978-1-966606-27-7

Acknowledgement

Without the support of Eastern Kentucky churches and businesses to assist both the Ramey Childrens' Home and the Boys Farm during my adolescent years, I would have had a very different childhood. I was very blessed to have been placed in an environment that gave me a chance to succeed in today's world. I would be remiss if I didn't give a lot of credit to Gertrude Ramey for my upbringing. She encouraged me to work hard, always giving your best efforts and trust in the Lord.

My career path was paved through determination and the many individuals who believed in me and my capabilities and I am forever grateful.

Adopting two infant children and raising them showed my wife and I that love is thicker than blood. Navigating life's twists and turns can be both exhilarating and exhausting, heartful and heartbreaking. Raising Caitlin and Chris taught us to treasure proud moments and hold on to precious memories.

I thank Debbie, my beloved wife of 44 years. Debbie has always made sure that I never doubted my capabilities and has been a positive driving force and my anchor. I am truly grateful for her input, edits and patience while I wrote and completed this book.

Most importantly, I thank God for his continued grace, guidance and blessings.

Dedication

Dedicated to abandoned, self-doubting children everywhere. Never give up for you matter.

About the author

Roger Ray was born and raised in the hills of Eastern Kentucky. Becoming of age, he enlisted in the U.S. Army, honorably serving his country during the Vietnam era, after which he began a dedicated Federal service career spanning over 25 years in the Nation's Capital area.

Roger also served as a Magistrate in the booming area of Loudoun County, Virginia before returning to his home state of Kentucky in 2005 with his wife, Debbie and their 2 children, Caitlin and Chris.

After a dozen years tending to their hobby farm outside Lexington, Kentucky, Roger and his wife now enjoy downsized living, attending their favorite church, walking their dog "Summer", playing pickleball, and traveling.

Table of Contents

Ashland, Kentucky

Just 11 months old, a baby boy and his 2-year-old sister were left in the care of an anonymous woman who lived on an Ohio River houseboat. The children's mom needed someone to look after the children while she attempted to land a job. Ten days later, with no word from the mom or indication that she planned on returning to retrieve her young children, the anonymous woman felt she had no choice but to surrender the 2 children to the Gertrude Ramey Children's Home.

That 11-month-old boy was me – Roger Ray - and this is my story.

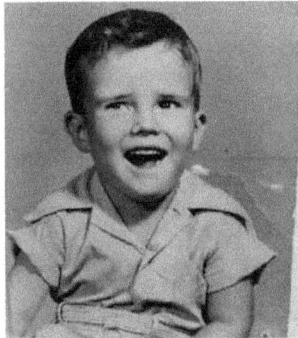

Roger

Young Nettie - Roger's Birth Mother

Gertrude Ramey
Children's Home

In 1944, a kind spinster woman named Gertrude Ramey from Salt Lick, Kentucky, began her life's mission of caring for Eastern Kentucky's abandoned children. A local boarding house, across the street from the Boyd County Courthouse, served as a haven for the overwhelming number of neglected, unwanted, and abandoned children entrusted to Gertrude's care. During the 1940s/1950s, there was no foster care or other avenue for neglected children unless a relative would take the affected children. The Courts were relieved and grateful for this woman named Gertrude Ramey.

"Welcome Home"

When brought to the Ramey Home along with my sister Linda, it was discovered that I had a 6-inch-long hernia in need of immediate repair. Dr. E.W. Jarrard performed the hernia repair operation. In later years, Ms. Ramey told me that I was having problems healing and remained confined to bed for a period of time. Evidently, it was very painful, so I cried a lot. When Dr. Jarrard visited the home to check on me, his prescription to help me heal was "Gertrude phenobarbital in a rocking chair".

During my years at the Ramey home, the number of children would average about 30 per day, though at one point in time, 51 children called it "Home". The initial Ramey Home was located at 2318 Winchester Avenue, Ashland, KY. The home was three stories with 14 rooms. Seven wide steps brought one to a massive porch supported by four stylish pillars. A big front door with large picture windows on each side and a semicircular window arching above the door welcomed visitors into the foyer. The second level had 3 double windows in front of each side of the house, stately brick chimneys rose from the ground, flanked by tall windows on both the first and second levels, separated by decorative brickwork. The smaller third level had three widow gables facing the street. It was about five or six feet back from the front side of the house, reaching up as if saying, "Now I'm finished". Inside were two fireplaces with dark-stained solid wood trim. The living room entryway was graced by two masts. The Ramey home cost $30,000 for the house, $22,500 for the land, and $7500 for repairs. The first floor held a combination dining and recreation room, a large reception and living room with new furniture provided by friends of the home, a modern kitchen, a food room, a large lavatory, and an isolation room furnished with hospital equipment made possible from local labor unions. The third floor had another large bathroom in the supervisor's room, and two boys' dormitories provided through a gift from Mrs. Henry W. Parlier. There was also a large storage space converted to temporary dormitory spaces. The Winchester Avenue House provided memories of good times of playing on the different levels with the other children.

Childhood at the Home

At just four years old, I was enrolled at Means Grade School on Carter Avenue, approximately 6 blocks from the Ramey Home. For the first 5 ½ years, I was never late nor tardy. The teachers were great; I was a good student and enjoyed school. I still remember my teachers' names – 1st and 2nd grade was Ms. Jennings; 3rd grade was Ms. Johnson but sadly she committed suicide that year (something no 3rd grader should try to understand); 4th grade was Ms. Wiesenberger (who I considered the best teacher ever even though I did need to call and apologize to her for any of my misbehavior); 5th grade Ms. Forsythe, and 6th grade Ms. Shute for just half the year as I was transferred from the Ramey Home to the Boys Farm. I remember when I was about 9 years old – I did something wrong while in the 4th grade, and Gertrude found out. She told me to go outside, get a switch, and then whipped me for being bad. Afterwards, she told me to go sit in a chair and stay there until I was allowed to leave. I told Gertrude that you can't punish someone twice for the same crime. I was quoting from the Magna Carta that I had recently read in the library.

Ashland Independent Article 1957

In 1954, the home received a collie dog with brown and white markings after a fence had been installed by Armco Steel Corporation, which is how the dog was named Armco. I became very attached to Armco, and his job was to keep me from straying from the house. One day, while I was playing with Armco, Ms. Ramey shouted, "Don't let him climb the fence". I decided to put her to the test. With her back turned, I started climbing the fence. Armco grabbed hold of my pants and would not let me go.

Ramey Children

Linda Ray, Bonnie White, Roger Ray

At that time, there were about 7 or 8 of us who, per court order, spent our adolescence at the home. My sister, Linda Ray, whom I learned years later was my half-sister, though I have always considered her my full biological sister. Bonnie White, who later changed her name to Bonnie Blue. Betty Jane, aka "Stinky"; Anita Clounch and her brother Ricky; Betty Joe, who ended up living at the home for over 40 years, helping Gertrude and Sandy Campbell, who also spent most of her years living at the Ramey Home. We were all expected to complete chores around the house. I was required to make my bed, brush my teeth, and take out the trash. The best assignment I was given was to get bread for the home from Betsy Ross bakery. I was given $.15 to ride the bus to the Bakery, which was about a mile and a half down on Winchester Avenue. My entrepreneurial self decided it would be best if I walked to the Bakery via the Dairy Cheer, where that $.15 would buy me an ice cream cone. With an ice cream cone in hand, I walked to the Betsy Ross Bakery, picked up 24 loaves of bread in a new bread box, and then the Betsy Ross staff called a cab for me to take the bread box back to the Ramey Home. Sweet Tooth happy and mission accomplished.

At home we were not allowed to watch television, read comic books or listen to the radio except when it was controlled by Gertrude or the staff. I was allowed to play Little League baseball for a short time, but I had no one to take me to the park for practice or games. I remember being allowed to join the Cub Scouts, which exposed me to other households and their family life. I particularly liked that they could watch cartoons, drink soda, and eat potato chips, so I did not mind walking the mile or so to our Cub Scout meeting, knowing that sodas and chips would be enjoyed at the end. In the fourth grade, I started staying late after school, going to the bowling alley to watch television or to the Paramount movie theatre, which allowed Ramey children to attend for free. I would often stay at the bowling alley for hours after school, watching TV in the nursery because no one bothered me. When asked where my parents were, I would say they were on lane eight.

As I never received an allowance from the Ramey Home, I was always looking for ways to make money. The Home was next to Nelson's Grocery Store, and Mr. Nelson owned several pieces of property beside his store with small yards and he would pay me $.10 per yard to mow. I cut the yards with a push mower and the $.10 Mr. Nelson paid me made me feel like the richest person in the world.

My entrepreneurial self also discovered that I could get into the Paramount Movie Theater, where the snack bar attendant would fill up a brown paper bag for me with popcorn. I would then take the bag of popcorn into the theater, find empty popcorn boxes, fill them with my popcorn, and try to sell the boxed popcorn. I could usually make at least $.50 whenever I went to the theater. Around the 5th grade, I would take classmates to the movies for free and charge them $.15 for popcorn. The theater was about eleven blocks from the Ramey Home, but I considered it a second home because of the "perks" it offered. I'd return home around 9-10:00 PM, sneaking back into the house and up to my 3rd-floor bedroom. When Gertrude found out what I was doing, she began locking me in my room at about 8:00 PM. Being alone on the 3rd floor by myself was very frightening at times.

Gertrude became wise to my sneaking around and would occasionally catch me slipping back into the house, which earned me a good spanking with a paddle, switch, or belt. I got so bad about not coming home that she eventually put me on a cot beside her room so she could keep track of my comings and goings.

I remember being asked a lot of questions when I first started school about why I lived at the Ramey Home, and that made me realize that I didn't know what a "real" family was. I was teased in grammar school about living at the Home and asked about my parents, so I made up stories about my Dad being killed in the Korean War and my Mom dying in a car accident. Sometimes kids tried to bully me about living at the Home, which made me want to fight back. In grade school, I became very self-conscious about being an orphan. Even with the care I received at the Home, I never felt that I had unconditional love. I don't recall ever being told by anyone that they loved me at the Ramey Home or the Boyd County Boys' Farm.

First White House Visit

On June 5, 1958, Gertrude Ramey, 3 Ramey Home girls, and I left for a trip to Washington, DC, and New York City. The trip included a luncheon with former First Lady Eleanor Roosevelt at her New York home. Our transportation was provided by the C&O passenger train that went through West Virginia's New River Gorge, passing the infamous Greenbrier Resort in White Sulphur Springs, Clifton Forge, across the Potomac River into Washington, DC, and finally to New York City.

At the luncheon with Mrs. Roosevelt, we were served chicken soup, cold cuts, vegetables, and iced tea. After lunch, Mrs. Roosevelt asked each of us if we had any questions. I recalled her conversing about her trip to Russia and sincerely asked what the conditions in Russia were. She told me that she was only shown the better sights while visiting and that she was not able to see much of what she would have liked to see about the real conditions there. She also told us that her husband, former President Roosevelt, often wished he could have turned a magic key to stop all the suffering in the world.

Mrs. Roosevelt wanted to hear from each of us, so we took turns telling her about ourselves. She confided that as a young girl, she was referred to as an "ugly duckling". Before leaving New York, we were able to see the United Nations Building, Radio City Music Hall, and the Empire State Building from the 86th floor. I recall that the buildings were enormous and the New Yorkers walked and talked very fast!

Then we went to Washington, DC, to visit and stay with Ms. Ramey's brother, Harry Ramey, who worked at the US Patent Office. While in Washington, we visited the White House, where President Dwight D. Eisenhower and First Lady Mamie Eisenhower were in residence. We were given a tour of the White House, where I was even allowed to sit in the President's chair in the Oval Office. I told Ms.

Ramey that since Mrs. Roosevelt said I could be President one day, I just wanted to try out the chair.

GETTING READY for a trip to New York and Washington are four children at the Ramey Children's Home and Miss Gertrude Ramey. Left to right are Betty Jane Sullivan, Miss Ramey, Sandra Campbell, Mary Ying and Roger Ray. (Staff Photo by Donithan)

★ ★ ★   ★ ★ ★

Gertrude Ramey, 4 Children Leave For 'Dream' In Capital, New York

By BURL OSBORNE
Independent Staff Writer

"This must be America," Miss Gertrude Ramey said thoughtfully as she and four of the children at her home prepared this morning to leave for a weekend dream that includes lunch with Mrs. Eleanor Roosevelt and a tour of the White House at the invitation of President and Mrs. Eisenhower.

The trip, which started at 3 p. m. when she and the children boarded a train for New York, is the result of three entirely unrelated situations.

First, the children at the Ramey Home for more than two years have wanted to take a trip, Miss Ramey said. They have saved allowances, sold candy and engaged in various other activities in order to raise money for the trip.

Miss Ramey said the children have always expressed a desire to see the Statue of Liberty and the Empire State Building.

The luncheon with Mrs. Roosevelt is a result of about a year of personal correspondence, Miss Ramey said. The head of the Ramey Home said she has written Mrs. Roosevelt a few times concerning social problems.

When the wife of the late FDR heard of their plan to visit New York, she wrote to the Ramey Home, inviting Miss Ramey and the children to have lunch with her.

The tour of the White House is an outgrowth of Miss Ramey's efforts about a year ago to prevent the deportation of a Mexican youngster, Mercedes Cota.

Miss Ramey wrote to the President in an attempt to see justice done, although technically the little girl should have been deported.

Discussing the President's helpful answer to her letter, Miss Ramey said with typical humility, "The Russians may have invented Sputnik first, but nowhere else in the world can the highest in the land meet with the lowliest on a common ground—this is a democracy."

Correspondence with the White House after the incident led to an invitation some time ago for the Washington visit.

Miss Ramey and the four—Betty Jane Sullivan, Sandra Campbell, Mary Ying and Roger Ray—will tour New York tomorrow evening, lunch Thursday with Mrs. Roosevelt, go to Washington Friday, and to the White House Saturday.

They probably will be back Sunday or possibly Monday, Miss Ramey said.

Ramey Children Washington, DC, and NY Trip 1958

Back at the Ramey Home

Ms. Ramey was able to hire a staff consisting of a cook (Ms. Childers) and a handyman (Mr. Stumbo) for small repairs around the house. During my years at the Home, the number of children would probably average around 30 per day. Gertrude and her staff were very limited in the attention that could be given to the children on a one-on-one basis. With the age range being infants to 17 years, it was incumbent upon the older children to help care for the younger ones. The Home always relied on the community, especially churches, to help with finances and food to keep it running. We went to church several times per week to learn the Gospel of Jesus Christ. The main message I always heard was that Jesus loved me. When you have never had anyone tell you they loved you, but you keep hearing that Jesus Christ does, it gives you a feeling of finally being wanted in life without judgment.

I remember the older girls giving me baths when I was around 5 or 6 years old, and they would often compete to see who should give me the next one. On more than one occasion, I was encouraged to perform inappropriate touching of a few older girls. I became a confused young boy who was really trying to figure out what females were all about. I was found a couple of times with girls my age in the bathroom playing "show me yours," and I'll show you mine".

Although I was never told that was the reason, I was eventually sent to the Boyd County Boys Farm because the home was afraid that when I reached puberty, it would be a real problem if I got one of the girls pregnant. Looking back, I'm sure that's the reason I had to leave the Ramey Home.

Make no mistake, I loved Gertrude Ramey. I always felt that I was one of her favorite children. I was like the poster boy for the home, as evidenced by the Ashland Daily Independent newspaper featuring my picture many times in stories about the Home.

1957 Christmas Shopping trip

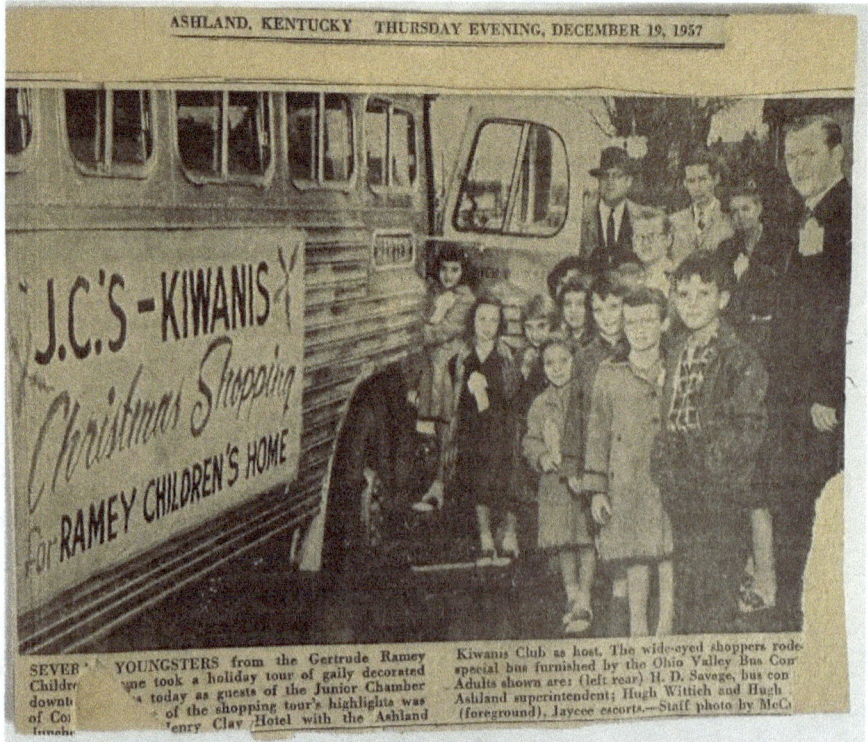

1957 Kiwanis

Good at Math but No Banker

I was so bad about not coming home on time that Ms. Ramey decided to send me to Hazel Green Academy, a boarding school in Wolfe County, Kentucky. This was the beginning of my fifth grade, and the boarding school allowed older students to smoke in an area designated for them. This was where I learned how to smoke a cigarette. The school was very nice, and I was even elected 5th-grade Class Treasurer, with the primary duty to collect 5 cents from every student each week for the treasury. Having never received an allowance, the temptation to spend this money as I wished was too great. When it came time for our Christmas party, there was no money in the treasury, and I was expelled from Hazel Green for taking the money.

A Farm in Rush

At around age 11, I was sent to the Boyd County Boys Farm in Rush, Kentucky, in a holler called Pigeon Roost. It was out in the boondocks, about 20 miles from Ashland and approximately three or four miles from the nearest store. My placement at the Boys Farm kept me from running the streets of Ashland, which probably kept me from becoming a much different person than who I am today.

The Boyd County Boys Farm was set up to provide a home for neglected and orphaned boys. The home consisted of a living room, dining room, kitchen, laundry room, indoor bathroom, and outhouse. The farmhouse attic had been converted into two rooms, each holding eight cots. We were expected to be up at 6:00 AM every morning, make our beds, do our chores, and if school was in session, be ready when the bus arrived. I did NOT like the Boys Farm.

The farm was started by Hack Estep, who was the Boyd County jailer at the time. He hired a couple, Mike and Shirley, who had a ten-year-old son named Steve. They were cruel and sadistic from my very first day there. They would beat you if you crossed them in any way. I was probably treated better than most of the ten or so boys (of various ages) housed at the farm at that time. Mike would discipline us with his belt on our backsides, and once I saw him tie a boy named Charlie to a tree and beat him with a board for wetting his bed.

That spring, I was allowed to go back to the Ramey Home to visit my sister Linda. I showed Linda my back, which was black and blue from some of the whippings I had received. I didn't know that Linda told Ms. Ramey about it. The next thing I knew, I was back at the Ramey Home while they looked for a new couple to run the Boys' Farm.

Hack Estep hired Harry and Susie Fowler to run the farm. Harry and Susie were nice people and managed the farm reasonably well. We still had discipline, but nothing like the heavy hand of Mike and

Shirley. The farm was a 120-acre property with a barn that housed chickens, cows, horses, and pigs. All the boys were responsible for taking care of the animals and for canning food from our garden for the winter. We often put up fences, which was very tiring, and I was also tasked with making lunch for prisoners from the county jail who were helping to build a new home for the farm.

The farm usually had about ten to sixteen boys. Very few of us stayed permanently; most were pass-throughs who were there because of neglect. The work was hard and demanding at times, but I do believe it built character and discipline in all of us. My main chores were taking care of the hogs and cleaning the house. I also helped tend the garden where we grew tomatoes, cucumbers, lettuce, potatoes, and green beans, which we canned whatever possible for the winter months. The hardest job on the farm was stripping fence posts, soaking them in fifty-gallon drums of creosote, and then digging holes to place the posts. Stringing barbed wire from post to post was not a job I'd wish on anyone.

The boys' farm had some interesting individuals, including the Walker and Prater brothers. I remember one boy who was a bit unhinged and was not allowed to eat at the dining room table because he had once tried to penetrate a cow while standing on an orange crate. It was also amusing to have visitors at the farm so we could show them around, especially the rabbit cages where the rabbits were always "busy". The looks on people's faces were well worth the tour.

We also had a horse named Scout that visitors enjoyed riding. However, Scout had a habit of taking riders down to the nearest tree and trying to knock them off. Our pony, Tony, would try to bite anyone who rode him. Guest visits were certainly not boring.

One of the saddest days on the farm was when Harry was bush hogging a field. Our dog, Whitey, who was pregnant, was lying in the grass about to deliver the pups when Harry accidentally ran over her and cut off her legs. She was in shock and screaming, and we had to put her down. Her pups also perished – it was a very sad day. On another occasion, we almost lost our dog Brownie. We had bought some piglets for $10 to raise, and one of them got away. About seven months later, Brownie encountered the hog at the creek, and they got into a fight. The hog nearly killed Brownie, but we were able to free him and chased the hog away.

During my time at the boys' farm, I didn't know that my sister Linda had been complaining to Gertrude about not being able to have much contact with me, except for a phone call every couple of months. Eventually, the boys' farm and the Ramey Home decided to allow me to be with Linda at a boarding school called Riverside Christian Training School. I enjoyed the school very much, though I did eventually get expelled from there also. One morning in the dorm, a high school junior named Jimmy made some nasty remarks about my sister. Being in the eighth grade and feeling brave to defend my sister's "honor", I decided to take him on, and we got into a fight. Unfortunately for me, he knocked out one of my front teeth, so once again I was expelled. When I got back to the boys' farm, I was taken to a dentist who fitted me with a partial plate for the front tooth I had lost. I could easily flick this tooth out with my tongue whenever I wanted. The tooth was shorter than my others, and I was very self-conscious about it for many years. That expulsion hurt more than my mouth, as at Riverside Christian, I was allowed to play sports. As an eighth grader, I played on the high school basketball team. Basketball was always my outlet when I was upset or depressed. After that "knock out" incident, I returned to the boys' farm and was sent to Cannonsburg School to finish the eighth grade. Cannonsburg had an outhouse with about 12 seats for the boys and coal stoves in the classrooms, which needed to be tended all day. I eventually settled into Cannonsburg and prepared myself for high school at Boyd County High.

Grateful for the Kindness of Strangers

Whether I was at the Ramey Home or the Boys Farm, I would often hear rumors about my real name. From a very early age until the sixth grade, my hair was cut at Todd's Barber Shop on Blackburn Avenue, Ashland. Mr. Todd would ask me how I came to live at the home, and he would tell me he heard my real name was Ricco. He was always very kind and never charged me for the haircuts. Years later, his son Jim Todd asked for assistance in helping his son with his employment goal, and I was grateful that I was able to do this favor for a family that showed much kindness to me over my childhood years.

School Days

I had a lot of mixed feelings during my school years about being wanted or loved. I was passed around, and I understand why, as I was somewhat difficult to control. I know that most of the people who had charge of my life did the best they could under the circumstances. Later in life, when I discovered that I had been lied to about my background, it affected me in ways that are difficult to explain. People I trusted who had lied to me probably believed they were acting in my best interest, but it caused even more insecurities than I already had. I can't say whether I would be any different today if I had known the truth back then, but I do know I have been very blessed. I truly believe Jesus Christ has watched over me, guided me, and prepared me for the world.

My high school years at Boyd County High were uneventful. My daily routine at the Boys' Farm was to awaken at 6:00 AM, slop the pigs, milk the cows, eat breakfast, and then wait for the school bus. The ride to school was about one hour, with two stops at other schools. At the end of the school day, my routine would be reversed, returning to the farm around 4:30 PM, where I did my assigned chores, prepared for dinner, did homework, and got ready for bed.

I really wanted to play sports in high school, but because of the distance and having no transportation, I was unable to. In the spring of 1966, I decided I couldn't finish school without playing a sport, so I tried out for the baseball team and made it. The long walks and difficulty getting rides from school to home didn't matter to me, and baseball turned out to be my best high school experience.

I don't recall ever taking books home to study because after chores and dinner, we were sent to our rooms until bedtime, which was between eight and nine o'clock. Occasionally, a friend from school would pick me up to go to a football or basketball game. Over my four years in high school, this happened maybe six times.

I recall my friend Larry Ferguson picked me up at the farm for a double date with Donna White and Brenda Ross. We were to meet at Donna's house and play games. Larry suggested that I take Donna for a ride in his dad's car. I had no driver's license at that time, but still jumped at the offer. Unfortunately, Donna didn't have a good time because, as I had never driven at night before, I was so excited and focused on being careful with the car that I basically ignored her. Still, what a thrill!

I did find myself in trouble in high school when I got into a fight with another boy on our school bus going home. We got off the bus and fought to a "draw," but we were reported to the school for fighting. When called to the principal's office, we were given a choice of three days' suspension or three swats with a paddle. I told the principal, Cobbie Lee, that I had no choice but to take the paddling. The other boy chose suspension. Those three swats were probably some of the most painful I've ever received.

After high school, I decided to attend Ashland Community College to pursue higher education. The Vietnam War was on at that time, and many students stayed in school to avoid being drafted. Post-graduation, I was able to get a summer job at the Federal Correctional Institution in Summit, Kentucky. They paid $1.25 per hour. My job was to assist the classification and parole office in admitting and discharging federal prisoners. The work was fascinating, and I enjoyed it very much.

I had bought a 1954 Ford for $100 from Harry Fowler. It was a rust bucket-you had to push it to start, and it had no floorboard to speak of. You could see the road as you drove. This was the car I used to go back and forth to school from Rush, KY, to Ashland, KY, about 20 miles each way.

I vividly recall taking my driver's test in that rust bucket 1954 Ford at the county courthouse. The state trooper who administered the test didn't seem happy to get into that car. When I told him that nothing worked and that I'd be using hand signals, he said, "ok". We drove out of the courthouse parking lot and went up a hill. He then told me to park as if I was leaving the car overnight on the hill. I did so, but didn't turn the car off. He asked why I left it running, and I explained that I'd have to push to restart it.

He then instructed me to go to the bottom of the hill, where there was a stop sign. I stopped, but he told me to return to the courthouse because I failed the test. When I asked why, he said I didn't make a complete stop. I argued that I had, explaining that there was no way I could get the car back into low gear without stopping completely. He still failed me.

When I got back to the courthouse, Hack Estep, the Boys' Farm founder, heard my story and offered to let me use his fairly new Chrysler De Soto to retake my driver's test the following week. This beauty had push-button transmission, power steering, and power brakes. When the officer got into the DeSoto, he was surprised to find that I was behind the wheel. As we drove out of the parking lot, I hit the power brakes for the first time and nearly sent the officer through the windshield. We circled the block, and he said, "You passed!" I was very grateful that Hack Estep loaned me the car.

I ran a roadblock once because it had no brakes. I was given a ticket for the violation and couldn't drive until it was fixed. I eventually sold my rust bucket Ford for $50. With all its faults, I still loved that car.

Four months before my 18th birthday, I got into a heated argument with Harry Fowler about the time I was spending at school, resulting in what he thought was too much time away from the farm and my chores. He became very angry, and I told him I would not take any more of his nonsense. Harry, who was in his sixties, had never seen me that angry. I scared him, and he claimed that I assaulted him, which I denied. There were no witnesses, but I made it clear I would no longer allow him to use his belt to discipline me. The Boyd County Sheriff arrested me for assault on Harry, and I was placed in the Boyd County Jail. I was held overnight without seeing anyone and was scared to death about what would happen to me.

Make or Break Time

The following morning, I was taken into Judge E.K. Rose's chambers and told that no charges would be pressed against me, but I was no longer welcome at the Boys Farm. I was forbidden to return to collect my meager belongings, though I was able to keep my car and the clothes on my back. The Judge suggested that I join the military and get on with my life.

I left the courthouse, and a deputy sheriff took me to retrieve my car. I had gotten to know some people at the Ashland YMCA, which had dormitory-style housing for railroad workers; basically, a 4X6 room with a cot and chicken wire over the top. It cost $1.00 per night, which allowed me to continue school, but I needed more money.

To make ends meet, I took on two additional jobs – one at a gas station and another at a Woolworth's store. I was working anywhere from 60 to 90 hours per week while still trying to keep up with college courses. It wasn't easy to keep up that pace, and I knew I needed to make some adjustments.

I ran into Lee, a friend with whom I had graduated from high school. He was also attending Ashland Community College and needed a roommate. Lee and I rented several apartments in Ashland, but unfortunately, we began hosting parties, which left me with less time for both work and school.

Uncle Sam Calls

Eventually, I met with the draft board about volunteering to join the US Army. I was advised that enlisting required a 3-year active-duty commitment, whereas being drafted would only require 2 years. I asked if I could volunteer for the draft and was told yes. Twenty-one months after leaving the Boys Farm, I was on my way to Ft Campbell, KY, as a member of the US Army. When I arrived at Ft Campbell, basic training was backed up because of the large number of volunteers and draftees. I, along with many others, was placed in a holding pattern until the next basic training class began. During that time, a Lieutenant approached me and said he wanted me to supervise a group of overweight draftees who were to fill sandbags daily, presumably as exercise. These men, about 12 or so, were some of the laziest people I had ever seen. On their very first day, they managed to fill maybe 100 bags. When the lieutenant returned at the end of the day and saw the minimal progress, he warned me that there had better be a lot more done the next day or I'd be doing the bags myself. That evening, I went into the barracks and told the men that tomorrow would be a different day. After breakfast the next morning, I grabbed a shovel, slammed it against a post inside the barracks, and told them to get their asses outside and start filling bags. I guess they thought I was crazy because they worked hard that day, unsure of what I might do if they didn't. When the lieutenant came back that evening, he was both pleased and impressed. I continued that assignment until the following week, when basic training officially began on April 1, 1968.

Roger U.S Army

We were all assembled in a field when several drill sergeants arrived, yelling loudly and calling us "soft shit birds". They shoved the recruits to get us moving toward the barracks to begin training. Thus began 12 weeks of intense physical and mental conditioning. For some reason, they tried to recruit me as an officer candidate, which required a six-year commitment. Upon successful completion, I would have been commissioned as a second lieutenant. However, I had learned that second lieutenants were "a dime a dozen" in Vietnam, so I had no interest in serving six years just to hold that rank.

My main drill sergeant was Sergeant Jose Santiago. He was not an imposing man physically, but you could tell he was not someone to mess with. Each morning, when Sergeant Santiago had us in formation, he would ask if anyone in the company wanted to take him on one-on-one before breakfast. No one ever accepted that offer. After formation, we would go on a 1-mile run, followed by the monkey bars. Then we could have breakfast, but only after everyone in the company had completed both the run and the bars—Many of the guys in basic training struggled to adjust to the barracks environment where they couldn't question or second-guess any request or command. I thrived in that environment, loving the competition that basic training provided, which pushed us to be the best we could be.

One of the basic training programs was using the Pugil stick. They were planning to film a training video demonstrating the proper way to handle the Pugil stick, and I was asked to represent C company in the competition. I was thrilled to be selected and eager to represent my company. I was matched against a Private from A Company. When the whistle blew, we went at each other, and in less than 25 seconds, he knocked me out. It happened so quickly that they decided to send in a backup to take him on. The replacement ended up having his ear bitten off by the same guy.

There were all kinds of men in basic training – some with college degrees, others high school dropouts; good family homes, others from difficult backgrounds. A few recruits were not allowed to participate in training involving hand grenades because they couldn't be trusted to follow instructions.

I enjoyed basic training. We had great food and excellent instruction in all aspects of warfare. When we graduated, and I was told I was being assigned to Military Police School at Ft Gordon, Georgia, I almost cried – as I loved basic training that much.

When I arrived at Ft Gordon, it was hot, humid, and a completely different atmosphere from basic training. The officers and sergeants treated you with respect and dignity, and they expected the same from you. They required you to complete your schoolwork as well as the physical training assigned. I ended up enjoying this aspect of military life just as much as basic training. This training required far more mental effort, especially in understanding the Uniform Code of Military Justice. The police training was excellent, and the overall experience was good. Upon completing my training, I received orders to report to Ft Bragg and prepare for deployment to Vietnam.

I took a 30-day leave, went back to Ashland to visit my girlfriend and her family, and then reported to Ft Bragg. To my surprise, I was charged with being AWOL for one day because I reported one day late. I was fined one day's pay for the offense. I was then informed that my orders for Vietnam had been canceled and that instead I was being sent to Ft Meade, Maryland, due to civil unrest across the country. The 519th Military Police Battalion was being activated to assist with riot control. There was widespread unrest following the assassinations of Martin Luther King, Jr, and Robert F. Kennedy, along with anti-Vietnam War protestors. As an MP in the 519th, we practiced riot control daily for several months. We were then deployed to Washington, DC, multiple times to assist with riot control.

Normally, we were stationed at Ft Belvoir, VA, before heading to our assigned locations in Washington, DC. I vividly remember being in my jeep at Dupont Circle with live ammunition for a .50 caliber machine gun mounted on the vehicle and sealed orders that could only be opened by the command of an officer. That was a heavy responsibility for a 19-year-old who loved his country and hated to see it torn apart. When we weren't engaged in riot control, the 519th conducted demonstrations on riot control tactics for police departments across the nation. These exercises took place at Ft Belvoir, where a mock city had been built. My company was always assigned the role of rioters. I would wear a blond wig, overturn cars, smash windows, and create chaos, making it challenging for the other MP companies to subdue the "professional rioters" from C company.

While stationed at Ft Meade, we also patrolled alongside the Anne Arundel County, Maryland Police, helping maintain order among military personnel in an area known as "Boom Town". We directed traffic on base, which also housed the National Security Agency, and conducted routine patrols daily.

One of the craziest things that happened to me occurred while I was on patrol. I was instructed to look out for a red pickup truck suspected of dealing drugs on base. If spotted, I was to pull the driver over and search for drugs on the person and in the vehicle. I was parked off State Route 197 when I saw the red pickup go by. My adrenaline surged as I took off in pursuit. The truck began speeding up, but I

27

stayed on its tail until it finally slowed down and pulled over. I exited my cruiser, ran up to the driver's side door, pulled the man out, pressed him against the truck, and spread his legs so I could search for weapons. To my surprise, he kept losing his balance and falling over. That's when I noticed he was missing a leg! For a moment, I thought I had kicked his leg off, not realizing it was prosthetic. When backup arrived, I retrieved the prosthetic leg, and to my even greater surprise, we found drugs hidden in the hollowed section. It was a wild experience and one I'll never forget.

Another of our duties as military police at Ft Meade was to assist in Ocean City, MD, where we were tasked with locating AWOL soldiers. I found out that AWOL soldiers were required to pay local and state officials for their capture out of their own pay.

Being a small-town "transplant", I found the social scene hilarious. I met some girls in Washington, DC, who worked for the FBI, and they were all roommates. They would invite some of their friends, and I would bring several soldiers from the 519th to parties almost every weekend. The roommates would call and beg me to bring more soldiers to their apartment building. These parties lasted for at least 15 months in high-rise apartment buildings in Alexandria and Arlington, VA. Show up with a 6-pack, and you're in for a lot of fun. When my best friend, Larry Homenick, got orders for Vietnam, it really put a damper on the parties.

Later in life, I was able to help Larry secure a job with the US Marshals Service, where he enjoyed a highly successful long-standing career. My battalion sergeant major, Al Jackson, later worked for me as a Deputy US Marshal. Additionally, several other friends from the 519th also had careers with the Marshals Service.

My Army active-duty service ended in March 1970. At that time, the military offered me a sergeant's hard stripe and $3,500 to sign up for an additional six years. At the time, I was a Specialist Class 4. The money offered was very attractive, but I had heard that the highest reenlistment bonus available was $10,000. I questioned why I was only being offered $3,500 and not the full $10,000. I was told I didn't have the required skill set to receive the larger bonus, to which I responded that if they gave me the higher amount, I would re-enlist. My request was denied, so I left the Army when my time was up.

Earlier, I rejected an offer to join the Washington, DC Metropolitan Police Department, which would have allowed me to leave the Army 6 months early. I turned that offer down because I didn't want to continue wearing a uniform. So, with no place to call home and no job waiting for me, I went to my sister Linda's house in Dayton, OH, to seek employment.

With the help of my brother-in-law, Jerry Huddleson, I got a job at GHR Foundry in Dayton. The facility produced parts for various industries. The work was hard, hot, and dirty, and I was working 40 to 50 hours a week and making fairly good money. After four months on the job, the company wanted me to enter management training.

One of my buddies from the 519th, Bob Brown, who later became an FBI Agent, would drive from Washington, DC, to pick me up on weekends and take me back to Virginia for some of those infamous high-rise parties. After doing this for several months, I decided to move to the Washington, DC, Metropolitan area and seek employment with the federal government. One of the girls, Maureen, who worked in a DC office, offered to let me stay at her place while I looked for a job. One of the first places I checked for employment was the Veterans Administration. They did not have any openings, but suggested I visit the US Marshals Service in Washington, DC, as they were hiring.

The U.S. Marshal for the District of Columbia at that time was Anthony Pappa. He had retired from the Pentagon as the Deputy Provost Marshal of the Army. He knew a lot about the 519th MP Battalion and had observed some of our demonstrations.

He swore me in that day as a Special Deputy U.S. Marshal and gave me a handwritten note stating as much. I could only work 39 hours a week, so I immediately sought to become a full-time Deputy United States Marshal. Upon inquiring with the Administration Office, I found out that I did not qualify under the Veterans' Readjustment Act, as it required you to be out of the military for less than six months.

I was advised that the only way I could become a Deputy United States Marshal at that time was to take the civil service test and get on the register. I did so and was later selected from the register to become a Deputy United States Marshal. I was hired as a GS-4 Step 9, earning about $6,000 a year. Other new veterans under the Veterans Readjustment Act were being hired at the GS-5, step 1, which paid slightly less than what I was earning.

Several Deputies filed an EEO grievance with the Marshals Service about the disparity in pay. Marshal Pappa asked if I would object to being moved to a GS-5, step 1, to resolve the grievance. He also assured me that he would help me recoup the lost wages through special assignments and other opportunities that might arise.

In my first year with the Marshals Service, I worked primarily in communications, specifically within the security unit. The U.S. Marshals Service had recently become an agency with the Director overseeing all 94 U.S. Marshals across the country. They were housed at 550 11th Street in Washington, D.C., and I spent a significant portion of my time in that building. I had frequent contact with the Director and his staff, which allowed me to become very familiar with them.

Wayne Colburn was the Director at that time. He was very personable and had a great attitude about everything. The 1972 Democratic Convention was held in Miami, Florida, and I was honored when the Director asked me to run communications for the Marshals' site in Miami. We were there for only a few days before the Democrats complained about our presence, prompting us to shut down that assignment.

During this assignment in Miami, I was awake 36 to 40 hours straight with no break. When Director Colburn found out how long I had been at the command site without rest, he insisted that I take his

Playboy Club card and go have a good time. I never used the card, as I was far too tired to do anything but sleep.

Once the Miami assignment was shut down, I returned to D.C. and was assigned to the U.S. District Court cell block. It was during this time that I met the man I would come to consider my dearest friend and confidant in the Marshals Service—Deputy U.S. Marshal David Murray. Everyone called him "Big Dave" because he stood about 6'6" tall and weighed around 260 pounds.

Roger & Big Dave

At the beginning of my cell block assignment, I was having a difficult time because we had to search all prisoners before court every morning. During a six-week stretch, I was averaging at least one encounter with a prisoner every week during the search process. I went to Dave and asked what I could do to keep this from happening so often.

Big Dave told me that because most of the inmates were Black, they thought I was being disrespectful by sometimes referring to them as "boy." I asked Dave what I should call them instead, and he suggested calling everyone "chief."

Everything went great for a couple of weeks, everyone was cooperative, and things ran like clockwork, until one day, one of the younger inmates told me to "f**k myself" and took a swing at me. Then it was on. Of course, with the manpower and security we had in the block, these outbursts didn't last long and were quickly brought under control.

When I told Big Dave what had happened, he asked me to point out the inmate who had started the disturbance. I pointed him out, and the next thing I knew, Dave was taking him down a corridor to a cell block at the back of the court elevator. When they came back to the main bullpen, Big Dave told me that I wouldn't have that problem again— and, to my surprise, I never did.

Dave later told me that he had advised the inmate that I was his brother and should be treated as such, or it could become a very serious problem.

One of our assignments was to transport prisoners across the country. These trips could last just a day or extend up to two weeks, travelling around the country picking up and dropping off inmates at different prisons and jails. I had taken several trips with many deputies over the years, but one that I will never forget was with a deputy named Hank.

This trip took us to Terre Haute, Indiana, for an overnight stay. Hank carried a .357 Smith & Wesson with a scope on the barrel and wore it in a wired holster on his hip. The local sheriff was quite impressed with Hank's personal weapon and asked if he would like to have a shooting contest the next morning. Hank was thrilled and couldn't wait.

We arrived early at the jail, hooked up our three inmates, placed them in the back seat, and followed the sheriff to a shooting range.

While the inmates cheered on Hank, Hank and the sheriff took about twelve shots each, with accuracy being the deciding factor in who won the shoot-off. Hank won by the slimmest of margins, but the inmates were very pleased.

Another incident involving Hank and his special scoped .357 occurred at the D.C. jail. When Marshals arrived at the jail, we were to place our weapons in a basket to be drawn up to the control tower, as they were disallowed in the institution. One day, as Hank and I were coming out of the jail and our weapons were lowered down for us to retrieve, Hank took his .357 Magnum and went to put it in his wire holster. Unfortunately, the trigger got caught on the holster's wire and discharged a shot, grazing Hank's buttocks. This caused quite a stir at the jail, but Hank and I had a good laugh about it.

Another deputy, Ed, was a delight to work with. He had so many stories—most of which were unbelievable—but he was good company on long trips. On one PC trip, after we had placed handcuffs and leg restraints on the inmates, we went on to explain what was expected of them during the journey. One inmate refused to be quiet. Ed had told him repeatedly to remain silent because he was disturbing everyone on the trip. After several attempts to get the inmate to quiet down, Ed pulled over, took the inmate out of the back seat, and escorted him to the trunk of the car. There, Ed opened it up, placed tape over the inmate's mouth, and put him in the trunk. It was probably the quietest trip I had ever been on.

Hank loved his CB radio, where his "handle" was "Bounty Hunter out of Watergate City." He would banter with truckers and women over long distances. He nicknamed me "the Kentucky Wild Child," his partner.

Later, in the fall of 1972, Marshal Pappa kept his promise by assigning me to a special duty assignment in the U.S. Virgin Islands, specifically Saint Croix, because of a massacre that had taken place at the Fountain Valley Golf Course. The Marshals sent a contingent of about twenty-five deputies to take over law enforcement duties on the island because the local police were not trusted. I rented a townhouse for my month-long stay that supposedly belonged to former Vice President Spiro Agnew.

Working with the local police was difficult because they all knew each other throughout the island and spoke a Cruzan dialect, which was difficult to understand.

This case was a racially motivated robbery and mass shooting occurring on September 6, 1972. Five local Black men invaded the Rockfeller-owned golf club, killing 7 White victims and 1 Black victim, wounding 8 others. The perpetrators were identified as Ismael LaBeet, Beaumont Gereau, Meral Smith, Warren Ballentine, and Raphael Joseph, some of whom had links to Black Power movements. After the robbery and murders, a massive manhunt involving local police, the FBI and US Marshals ensued leading to the arrest of all five suspects. All five men were convicted of murder, assault and robbery. All were sentenced to 8 consecutive life terms in Federal prison.

When this assignment concluded, I received a call from a high ranking official in the US Marshal's Service who asked what a bottle of rum cost in the US Virgin Islands. When I told him it was basically $1.00 per bottle, he asked if I would bring back 12 bottles for him to give as Christmas gifts. I purchased the 12 bottles and placed the rum in the gas masks crate going back to Headquarters in Washington, DC. All shipments arriving at Miami International Airport from outside the continental USA had to go through US Customs. I was questioned by Customs Officials as to why bottles of rum were inside the gas masks crate. I told them the truth about what I was doing. Unknown to me was that the head of Customs at the Miami Airport was the brother of the US Marshal official who had requested the rum. I was relieved that I was allowed to pass with just a warning and no incident report. The rum arrived safely to its destination.

Special assignment details could take a Deputy anywhere from the Caribbean Islands to the Plains of South Dakota, where I found myself in 1973 serving as Communications Specialist. For 71 days, about 200 Indians occupied Wounded Knee, South Dakota, holding off US Marshals and the FBI in protest of what they called a corrupt tribal government and the US government breaking treaties with the tribes.

Watergate City

After June 17th, 1972, when security guard Frank Willis foiled a break-in at the Democratic National Committee headquarters at the Watergate complex in Washington, D.C., things got very busy. It was like being on a special assignment for the next couple of years. I was assigned at various times to protect Judge John Sirica, his wife, and their daughter during the investigations and the trial known as Watergate.

Roger USMS

On one occasion, Judge Sirica was to receive the *Time Magazine* "Man of the Year" award and had to leave D.C. to accept it. Deputy Mason Ebhart and I were on protection detail at Judge Sirica's home, watching over Mrs. Sirica and their daughter. When we arrived at the residence, we were informed that it was the daughter's graduation night and that she would be hosting a party with friends that evening. Everything went smoothly until around midnight, when D.C. Metropolitan Police received a complaint about a loud noise coming from the residence. They showed up, with members of the press in tow, and wanted to know what was going on. We advised them that we had things under control, that their services would not be needed, and that we would ensure the music volume was lowered.

Not an hour later, the Metropolitan Police and press returned to the Judge's residence. At that point, Deputy Ebhart and I decided it was time for the party to end. We asked everyone to leave, and they did. The next morning headline in the Washington Post newspaper read, "Marshals Come to the Aid of the Party." I had to meet with Judge Sirica on Monday morning to explain the situation from the weekend. He stated that he fully understood and appreciated our attention to detail.

On another occasion, Judge Sirica called me into his chambers and handed me a box containing the Watergate tapes. He instructed me to carry these tapes to MIT in Boston to determine whether they had been altered or deliberately tampered with, or if they could be restored to reveal at least one 18½-minute gap on the tape. I took the tapes home that night to my apartment in Maryland and prepared for the trip. Using a government travel request for myself and the recordings, I set out for Boston.

When I arrived at the airport to take the Eastern Shuttle to Boston, I was pre-boarded because I was carrying a firearm. Once the plane was fully boarded, a stewardess approached me and told me I would have to place the box under the seat. I informed her that I had a paid receipt for the box and that it would not go under the seat but would remain beside me for the duration of the flight.

The stewardess left and soon returned with the co-pilot, who informed me that FAA regulations required the box to be placed under the seat. I told him that I had purchased a ticket for the box, it would remain in the seat beside me, and it was not going anywhere else. He was not pleased but left. Moments later, the pilot approached and told me the same thing—that the box had to go under the seat or he could not fly. I advised him that if he couldn't fly, they should find someone who could, because the box was not leaving my side.

Within five minutes, the plane began taxiing, and we were airborne. During the short flight to Boston, the stewardess returned several times, curious about the contents of the box. I told her that I was not at liberty to disclose or discuss what was inside. She smiled and kept teasing me about it whenever she passed. Eventually, I told her that once I had delivered the package, I would tell her what was in the box—but not until then.

It was clear she couldn't wait until my return flight to D.C., as I would be flying back on the same shuttle with the same crew. When I returned and took my seat, she rushed back to me, eager to know what had been in the box. I told her that once we were in the air, I would let her know. She could hardly wait. As soon as the plane reached altitude, she came straight to my seat. I told her, "It was the Watergate tapes." She said, "No way! You're BS-ing me! There's no way those were the Watergate tapes." I don't know if she ever believed me, but it was fascinating to see how people reacted—especially when I told them what had really been in that box.

The Watergate jury was sequestered for the entire trial. They were housed in hotel rooms with 24/7 security and were always escorted whenever they needed to leave their rooms, even for emergencies. We arranged movies for them, took them out to dinner, and hosted a lovely Thanksgiving celebration, a Christmas party, and a New Year's Eve party to break up the monotony of being sequestered for such an extended period.

I didn't mind working during the holidays, so I volunteered to work all of them with the jury. On New Year's Eve, the foreman of the jury, John A. Hoffar, a retired policeman with the National Park Service, requested to go for a walk near the hotel and the zoo to get some fresh air. I accompanied him, and during our walk, he mentioned that we were treating the jurors too nicely. He said they had been in deliberation for some time, and he had not been able to convince them to reach a verdict. However, he felt that now that the holidays were over and the parties had ended, with nothing left to look forward to but rendering a verdict, they would reach one soon. Sure enough, the very next day, they returned with a verdict. John H. Mitchell, the former Attorney General; H. R. Haldeman, former White House Chief of Staff; John D. Ehrlichman, former White House Domestic Advisor; and Robert C. Mardian, former Assistant Attorney General, were found guilty. Kenneth Wells Parkinson, a lawyer for Mr. Nixon's reelection committee, was found not guilty.

The last thing I remember about the Watergate investigation was the movie titled *All the President's Men,* based on the book written by Bob Woodward and Carl Bernstein. I was the duty officer for the U.S. Marshal Service in the District of Columbia one weekend when they needed assistance with continuous security. I don't recall the exact date, but I remember it was a Saturday. I was able to provide the film crew with Marshal Service credentials and information on how the arraignments and trials related to Watergate had been handled. I received the credentials back at the end of the day, and that marked the end of my involvement with the Watergate cases.

United States District Court
for the District of Columbia

Chambers of
Judge John J. Sirica

March 14, 1975

Mr. Roger Ray
Deputy United States Marshal
Washington, D. C. 20001

Dear Mr. Ray:

I want to take this opportunity to express to you my personal gratitude for your commendable service during the course of the Watergate proceedings.

By your fine service you are a credit to yourself, as a citizen, and to the office of the United States Marshal.

Sincerely yours,

John J. Sirica

Mr. Ray

United States District Court
for the District of Columbia

March 29, 1972

Chambers of
John J. Sirica
Chief Judge

Mr. Anthony E. Papa
United States Marshal for the
District of Columbia
United States Courthouse
Washington, D. C. 20001

Dear Marshal Papa:

During the recent trial of the Amidown case you detailed the following United States Deputy Marshals from your office to insure the safety and well-being of my family and myself for the duration of the trial: Charles S. Artley, Jack E. Braxton, Jr., Peter Craig, Carlton M. Ebhardt, Francis A. Hammer, Richard Oakorum, Roger Ray, Allen Ross, Herbert Spiller and Roy E. Welch. These deputies were most courteous and efficient in the performance of their duties and reflected most favorably on the United States Marshals Service in general and your office in particular.

In addition, Deputy United States Marshal Donald Waite, who was in charge of the jury during the case, rendered invaluable service in that regard.

I want you to know that I and my family are deeply grateful to all these deputies for their help and I would ask that you convey our thanks to them.

I would hope that a copy of this letter will be placed in the personnel file of the deputies named herein and I am taking the liberty of sending a copy of this letter to each of them.

Sincerely,

John J. Sirica

Letters from Chief Judge Sirica

A City of Two Judicial Jurisdictions

US Marshals Service served the U.S. District Court (Federal) and DC Superior Court (city)

D.C. Superior Court

I was assigned to Judge "Turkey" Thompson in D.C. Superior Court for a year as the Marshal responsible for coordinating courtroom security and ensuring that prisoners were always delivered on time for court. The Assistant United States Attorney assigned to prosecute cases in Judge Thompson's court was Joseph DiGenova.

Judge Thompson was a good judge and a good man. One comical thing he often asked me to do was serve as the best man for weddings held in his chambers. The newlyweds of these 15 or so weddings always got a kick out of having a Deputy U.S. Marshal holding the rings.

In another instance in Judge Thompson's court, a criminal trial was held for an individual who had shoplifted a ham from a supermarket and was caught leaving the store. As I recall, the defendant had a criminal history and was being charged with theft. At the beginning of the trial, Judge Thompson instructed the jurors to go to the jury room. Their first order of business was to select a foreman, after which they were to deliberate on the defendant's guilt or innocence.

This was a straightforward case that should have taken no more than two hours to select a jury foreman and render a verdict. After the third day, Judge Thompson asked me what I thought the problem might be. The deputy assigned to provide security for the jury during deliberations informed me that they seemed to be having difficulty selecting a foreperson. I relayed this to Judge Thompson, who had me bring the jury back into the courtroom to determine the holdup.

41

The jurors explained that they had not selected a foreman because no one had received unanimous support. Judge Thompson inquired about the vote count. One gentleman raised his hand and said the count was eleven to one. The judge didn't ask who had received the single vote, but the man said he had and that he felt the election wasn't fair.

Judge Thompson advised the jury that they needed twelve votes to select a foreman so that he would cast the twelfth vote. He then asked who had received the other eleven votes. A petite woman raised her hand and told the court that she had. Judge Thompson informed the court that she was now the forewoman and instructed the jury to deliberate and return with a verdict. No more than twenty-five minutes later, the jury returned with a guilty verdict.

The United States Marshal for the District of Columbia also served as the sheriff of D.C., performing duties that would normally fall under the sheriff's jurisdiction in other communities. The district was divided into seven areas, which coincided with the seven districts of the Metropolitan Police Department. I was assigned to both the Seventh District in Southeast as well as the Third District in Northwest, serving process and overseeing evictions.

Difficult evictions were probably the least desirable of our duties and the most dangerous. DC evictions were scheduled every day that it was not raining. Usually, there were 30 to 40 evictions scheduled per day. My typical day would include around 10 evictions, with me being the only deputy on scene. The landlord was required to provide a crew to meet me at a specific time to carry out the evictions.

I would secure the area by knocking on the door to see if anyone was home. If no one responded, I would have the landlord open the door so I could make entry, secure the dwelling, and then allow the landlord and his crew to remove everything from the premises and place it neatly on the curb. The premises were then turned over to the landlord.

The most surprising eviction occurred when Deputy Marshal Al Ross and I were conducting an eviction in an upper Northwest apartment complex, where the landlord had indicated there might be a problem. When Al and I arrived at the scene, I knocked on the door, but since no one answered, I had the landlord open the lock. Hearing loud music coming from the apartment, we asked the landlord and his crew to stay outside until we secured the premises.

I called out several times for anyone in the apartment to identify themselves and stated that we were U.S. Marshals there to conduct an eviction. We cleared the first floor, but I could still hear the music, and it sounded as if it were coming from upstairs. Al and I secured the first floor to make sure no one was there and finding it basically empty, we then went upstairs, where the music was blaring. We were very cautious because, although things seemed calm, situations could turn dangerous in an instant.

With guns drawn, we moved slowly up the stairs, Al behind me. The loud music continued. At the top of the stairs, a door was slightly open, and it seemed the music was coming from there. As I approached, I noticed a small crack in the first door on the left. With the barrel of my gun in front of me, I gently pushed the bottom of the door open a little wider so I could see inside the room.

I was so stunned by what I saw that I instinctively pulled back and accidentally knocked Al halfway down the stairs because of how close he was behind me. To my shock, a large woman was lying nude on the bed, wearing headphones and using a vibrator. It was only when we appeared in her doorway that she even noticed us. Naturally, we were all embarrassed, but afterward, Al couldn't stop laughing. We instructed her to get dressed, turn off the music, and leave the premises. She was not a threat, but as it turned out, she did not legally live there.

On another eviction, after no one responded to my repeated knocks and identification, I instructed the landlord and the eviction crew to remain outside until I cleared the premises. While checking the different rooms to ensure no one was present, I heard moaning and groaning coming from a back room. I proceeded to that room and found a man lying on his bed with his right leg severely infected.

As I spoke to him, he told me he was a veteran trying to get disability benefits, that he was down on his luck, and had nowhere to go. I asked the landlord to call an ambulance to take him to the hospital for treatment, but the landlord refused. I informed the landlord that I would not evict the man and would call the ambulance myself to take him to the hospital. The landlord complained that he had a legal eviction scheduled and threatened to sue me and the Marshal's Service if I did not complete it.

I told the landlord that I would report the situation to the court. Once the court received my return explaining what had happened, no suit was filed. The court ordered that the eviction be reissued without cost to the landlord.

The only time that I ever arrested an individual on an eviction was the landlord. This was a fourth-floor apartment of a Northwest DC high-rise. The landlord and his crew arrived at the appropriate time, and I went to knock on the door, but received no response. I asked the landlord and the crew to stay outside. While I was checking the inside for any occupants, the eviction crew was getting some flak from some of the residents for going to evict the person who lived there.

I advised the landlord that I had only one hour for the scheduled eviction and that if his crew did not move, I would have to cancel it and he would have to reschedule. At that time, the landlord pulled a revolver and threatened to shoot the crew if they did not complete the eviction. I informed the landlord that his actions were ridiculous, and I subsequently arrested him on several charges. No eviction occurred at the residence on that day.

Another "memorable" eviction was at an apartment building on Rhode Island Ave, NW. When I arrived at the residence, the landlord and his crew were waiting. I noticed that across the street, there were probably eight to twelve residents sitting in lawn chairs, drinking, and watching what was going on. When I knocked on the door, there was no answer, so again, I had the landlord and his crew stay outside until I inspected the premises for anyone inside.

During evictions, part of the deputy's responsibility was to ensure that valuables or contraband (money, jewelry, alcohol, pornography) were not put on the curb. This residence had lots of furniture, personal belongings, and many items that needed to be removed. There was no one home, so there was no reason for the eviction to be canceled. I advised the landlord and his crew to begin taking everything to the street and to stack it neatly on the curb.

While they were moving things out of the residence and placing them on the street, I kept watch on the property removal and the crowd across the street. I noticed from the upstairs window that a woman from the group took a chair and walked it over to her side of the street. When I came downstairs to retrieve the chair, she ran with another chair on her back, holding it with her hands. I grabbed one of the chair legs, she let go, and stumbled into a telephone pole, causing a head gash that bled profusely.

The other residents across the street then began shouting threats at me and coming toward me. I retreated into the building where the eviction was taking place, but it was not going to continue until I had reinforcements. The Metropolitan Police Department's Special Operations Group responded to my request for backup, and I was then able to complete the eviction. I did not arrest or charge the lady for taking the chair during the eviction, on the condition that she return it, which she agreed to, and everything turned out okay when it could've been a catastrophe.

U.S. District Court

The U.S. District Courthouse cellblock during the early 1970s averaged about 150 prisoners a day. We received an additional 100 or more from the Metropolitan Police Department who were locked up the night or weekend before. Jail runs would start around 5:30 or 6:00 a.m., with vans and a bus to the D.C. Jail, the Women's Detention Center, the Juvenile Detention Center, and Saint Elizabeths Hospital (mental institution) to pick up inmates for the day. The bus was usually staffed by two deputies and a driver. The bus would hold approximately 60 prisoners at a time, and we had vans that would carry anywhere from 10 to 12 prisoners at a time every morning, and then during the day, we would transport the prisoners back to the jail for the evening.

I was assigned to the District Court cellblock for about a year and a half, where I was given these duties early in the morning and throughout the day. When the prisoners arrived, they were searched and put in different bullpens depending on their status or the courts they would be attending on that day. These individuals were involved in mental health hearings, arraignments for various crimes, serving as witnesses in cases, and were on trial for various criminal offenses. Our duties included ensuring the production of all prisoners for that day and delivering them to the proper courtroom, interview room for attorneys, or to the Grand Jury.

Pretrial Services also had to drug test all the prisoners before being arraigned that day, and they were interviewed for the possibility of receiving bond or having their case dismissed. This was before the District of Columbia got Home Rule, and therefore, the majority of those incarcerated came to the United States District Court for the District of Columbia. Later, when DC received Home Rule, most DC inmates and new arrestees were taken to DC Superior Court rather than US District Court. The Superior Court consisted of several different buildings that housed certain jurisdictions over different circumstances that came to the court each day.

The U.S. District Court was much easier because it was all in one building. In Superior Court, we had an A Block, a B Block, a Juvenile Block, and a Female Block. These were all separate buildings manned by a different setup of Deputy U.S. Marshals. I would be assigned to one of these blocks on different occasions, and it was quite dangerous in how we had to transport prisoners to the proper courts. In some cases, we would have to walk juveniles on the street to their assigned courtrooms because there was no cellblock in the Juvenile Court. On other occasions, we would find inmates who needed to go to Building B, and they would have to be walked in the street as well. This was not an ideal situation and was very dangerous over the years.

Two weird but memorable incidents that occurred while I was assigned to the United States District Court for the District of Columbia are: There was an inmate from Lorton Penitentiary who was on trial before Judge June Green for murdering another inmate at Lorton. The inmate, Willy Joiner, stabbed and killed another inmate and was trying to claim that he was mentally insane at the time, and even during his trial, that he was mentally impaired.

During the trial, when Willy was in court, he would act kind of stupid and out of it, but when he came back to the cellblock, he seemed very normal. Unbeknownst to anyone, one day during lunch break, Willy took the lunch bag, defecated in it and put the bag in his pants before going back to the trial that afternoon. I took Willy up to Judge Green's courtroom through the back elevator of the courtroom and dropped him off with the courtroom deputy. It wasn't twenty minutes later that the alarm went off in the courtroom. Several deputies and I sprinted to the elevator, arriving at the courtroom in under a minute.

Upon opening the door, we were met with a scene of feces scattered everywhere. It was all over the courtroom bench. Willy was on the floor being held by the deputy assigned to him during the trial. We took Willy back to the cellblock, and he reverted to his old self, stating he didn't want any problems; he just wanted the judge to know that he was crazy. Several weeks later, Internal Affairs interviewed me about why I did not smell anything when I took Willy up to court. After the investigation, I was found not to have done anything wrong, but the lunch procedure was changed. Inmate lunch from then on was still a sandwich and a piece of fruit, but no bags.

The saddest day that I had as a Deputy United States Marshal in the District of Columbia was on September 24, 1971. A Deputy United States Marshal was shot and killed while guarding a prisoner who was attending his father's funeral. The prisoner's brother was able to disarm marshals guarding the prisoner in the back of the Florida Avenue Baptist Church. The brother and the prisoner attempted to escape from the church, but Deputy U.S. Marshal Norman Sheriff confronted them. The suspect opened fire on the marshal, killing him. The prisoner and his brother were stopped about two miles from the incident and were taken into custody, convicted of the murder, and sentenced to life in prison. During this incident, I was working in the communication center and coordinating the case as it was ongoing until the successful apprehension of the murderers.

Around 1973, I was elected vice president of Local 2272 of the American Federation of Government Employees (AFGE). The president, Charlie Burgess, tasked me with handling negotiations with management regarding the rotation of deputies across the various sections of the D.C. Marshal Service. They included the Warrant Squad, District Court, Superior Court, Cell Blocks, Process, and Prisoner Transportation nationwide trips. This exercise in meeting with management and negotiating for the deputies was helpful in preparing me to later become a Supervisory Deputy United States Marshal. I applied for probably 75 to 100 open positions around the country during this time to become a Supervisory Deputy United States Marshal.

In 1974, I met a beautiful girl in the US District Court cafeteria who worked in the U.S. Probation Office, primarily doing presentence reports. She let me know that she had done the reports on the Watergate defendants before their sentencing. Her name was Debbie Callahan. We began dating, becoming very close in a short time, enjoying life in the DC Metro area. As VP of the AFGE, I asked Debbie if she would be willing to type reports involving Local 2272, and she agreed, though the pay was minimal at $1.50 per page. Ironic but true – AFGE Local 2272's small office was in none other than the Watergate Hotel, where the infamous DNC break-in had taken place years prior.

Debbie and I would visit the Fraternal Order of Police (FOP) Lodge One in Washington on a regular basis, where we had lots of friends. I was sent as a FOP Lodge #1 delegate to the National Convention in Nashville, Tennessee, with several others. Debbie and I always enjoyed playing pinball over beers with other law enforcement officers from the Metropolitan DC community. Though we had absolutely no idea how to ski, we signed up for the Lodge's annual Pennsylvania ski trips. We learned very quickly that we did not have the proper ski slope attire, needed to learn the skill of getting on and off the ski lift and snowplowing down the slopes would be our best friend. Though embarrassing at the time, we are grateful we never sustained injuries and enjoyed many laughs with law enforcement buddies while in the beautiful Pocono Mountains.

One day, to my surprise, Debbie invited me to a Washington Redskins football game. I did not know at that time that she was a "Redskinette," the Redskins cheerleading squad, performing during the Redskins home games at RFK Stadium. I was always a Cleveland Browns fan, but quickly changed to a Redskins fan after going to the games with Debbie. Much different from today, at that time, two game tickets were the only compensation received by the cheerleaders. When the Washington Redskins won the 1992 NFC Championship against archrival Dallas Cowboys, the team and Redskinettes were headed to Pasadena, CA, for Super Bowl XVII. For eight years, I was the biggest Redskins and Debbie fan in both RFK Stadium and the Rose Bowl! The Washington Redskins beat the Miami Dolphins to become Super Bowl XVII Champions, after which Debbie decided 8 years was enough and she "hung up her boots" on that victory!

Debbie Washington Redskinette 1974 – 1983

Whether on or off the field, Debbie always remained my biggest cheerleader. She constantly encouraged me to continue applying for positions and keep the faith. That truly meant the world to me as I had no family to lean on, request advice, or even just say… You got this, Roger!

Though I remained confused about the circumstances of my abandonment at 11 months old and subsequent placement at the Ramey Home, I harbored no ill feelings toward Gertrude. When I reached adulthood and was on my own, I continued to stay in touch with Gertrude. Debbie and I visited the Home, treating the children to bowling, pizza, basketball, etc. It was my way of giving back to the place I knew as Home for many years. On one occasion in 1976, Gertrude called and informed me that she had received an invitation to visit the Gerald Ford White House along with some of the children in her care at that time. She inquired whether I might be able to help with the logistics, and I said, Of course. Gertrude, Dr. Robert French, Ella Galliher, and 13 Ramey children rode in a van from Ashland, KY, and stayed at my 3-bedroom home in Southern Maryland. Gertrude asked if I would accompany them on this White House visit, which would take place in July 1976. It was a private tour that exposed all of us to the history and beauty of the White House. Accommodating 16 people at my small home was no easy feat. Still, Gertrude, the children, and the adult chaperones thoroughly enjoyed Washington, DC, and even ate a local Maryland favorite – steamed crabs.

Ramey Children's visit the White House, July 1976

Ms. Ramey and Roger, July 1976 at Roger's Maryland Home

A F F I D A V I T

I, the undersigned, Gertrude Ramey, state that I am the Superintendent of the Gertrude Ramey Childrens Home in Ashland, Kentucky and have served in that capacity for approximately 35 years; that the following is a true and correct statement relating to the facts of the birth and early childhood of Roger Ray, who now serves as Deputy U. S. Marshall in the Washington, D. C. area; that Roger Ray was brought to the Gertrude Ramey Childrens Home, then located on Winchester Avenue in Ashland, Kentucky around October or November of 1949; that the affiant has personal knowledge that at that time Roger Ray was around eleven (11) months old; that the affiant recalls that she was given this information by either the Sheriff or a Juvenile Officer; that according to the information supplied Affiant the birth day of Roger Ray was November 22, 1948; that this information was transcribed on a written record, which written record was destroyed by fire several years ago.

The affiant further says that the birth day of Roger Ray was always celebrated on November 22 during the many years he resided in the home; that based on the affiant's personal knowledge as to the date of admission of the said Roger Ray at the Home, and his age at that time, that she can reasonably state that the official birth date of Roger Ray was November 22, 1948.

Witness:

Grace Clark

Deloris Bartley

Gertrude Ramey
Gertrude Ramey

Subscribed and sworn to before me by Gertrude Ramey this 30th day of March, 1978.

Sam F. Kibbey
Sam F. Kibbey
Notary Public
State-at-Large

SAM F. KIBBEY
My Commission expires May 14, 1979

Gertrude Affidavit

In 1976, I submitted my application and was selected for the Marshal Service's inaugural intern program for Supervisory Deputy United States Marshal. The US Marshals Service selected five individuals from across the country for a one-year internship learning all the Divisions of the USMS headquarters. During the year, we spent one month in each division (Finance, Operations, EEO, Building Security, Fugitive Investigation, Training, Budget, Special Operations, Prisoner Transportation, Witness Security, Communications, Human Resources, and Internal Affairs to understand the variances and tasks required to succeed in each of these divisions. The individuals selected for this inaugural program were Art Dixon, Terry Merrifield, Kent Pekarek, Richard Reynolds, and me.

Ron Pautz was charged with ensuring all interns completed and were proficient in every aspect of the program. The intern program allowed each of us to thoroughly learn the diverse divisions within the USMS. I really enjoyed this program very much, especially while at the Federal Law Enforcement Training Center (FLETC) in Glenco, Georgia, where I spent a month instructing new recruits. In one class, we were to instruct students on the proper use of restraint handcuffs, leg irons, waist chains, as well as arms, for securing prisoners during transportation.

It was decided that I would instruct the class on how to properly secure an individual with restraints for transport to or from court. Dick Reynolds and I discussed how we would proceed with this lesson. It was thought that I would secure Dick as if he were an inmate to be transported. They did not know we had decided to put a handcuff key up Dick's nose before doing the exercise. After I secured Dick with chains, handcuffs, and leg irons, I invited the students to come up and search Reynolds to see if he was securely handcuffed and unable to escape. When the students decided they had searched Reynolds thoroughly and he couldn't escape, I then told Reynolds, "Go ahead and escape if you can," and he replied, "Yes, I will show them how I can escape."

Reynolds then tried with all his might to push the key from his nose into his hand, but to no avail. It quickly became clear that the key was stuck. As a last resort, Reynolds turned his back to the students and blew as hard as he could, which caused the key, with bloody snot, to come out of his nose. The class burst into laughter at what had just happened. I must admit it was a very funny incident, though the class soon realized it could have had serious consequences if he had been a real prisoner, as all searches must be completely thorough to keep you and your partner safe.

Another training exercise at the academy involved acting as witness security protectees. Five students from the U.S. Marshal Service would protect a witness from 9 a.m. until 2 p.m. to produce the witness in court to testify. In my group, I gave the five trainees a tough time for most of the day. But after the time was up and they produced me in court at 2 p.m. to testify, they passed their test.

Unfortunately, in Dick Reynolds' group, they were not so lucky. Dick was a model witness from about nine to noon on that day. He complained to the trainees that he wanted something to eat for lunch, and he suggested that they go to McDonald's and have a sandwich. While at McDonald's, Dick said he needed to go to the restroom, so he left the table, headed to the restroom, and then started running out of McDonald's, going to the outside as if he was going to escape.

Unknown to the students and even myself, Dick had invited his wife Dora down to the Training Center and to take in the sights of the Jekyll Island area. Together, Dick and Dora devised a plan for Dick to escape from the deputies at the McDonald's. Their plan worked to perfection. The trainees were unable to produce the witness in court at 2:00 pm to testify. Again, the deputies learned a very valuable lesson: when individuals are in your custody, you must always have complete control of them to meet your responsibilities to the court and to ensure the safety of your charges.

That incident reminded me of a witness security assignment that I had several years prior in Boston, Massachusetts. The witness, whom

55

I'll call Vinny, was from New York and was testifying against one of the New York mob families. Vinny was very flashy, fast-talking, and antsy to move about town. Our cover at the motel where we stayed with Vinny was that we worked for the Environmental Protection Agency, checking on the water supply in the Boston suburbs. I had been on the detail for about three days when we received information that we needed to move immediately because of intelligence indicating he might be in danger.

When checking out of the motel, the front desk clerk said, "It must be pretty dangerous to check the water content." I asked, "What do you mean?" The clerk replied that Vinny told them he was a United States Marshal and was there to protect us from the environmental protests. I shared this information, along with the rest of the details, and advised Vinny that he could be arrested and charged with impersonating a United States Marshal.

I successfully completed the Intern program and, in 1977, was assigned as a supervisor in the Alexandria, Virginia, Marshal's Office. When the Chief Deputy retired, I applied and was selected as the Chief Deputy for Eastern Virginia, which encompassed Alexandria, Richmond, Norfolk, and Newport News, Virginia. The Marshals Office had four offices staffed by approximately 80 employees (Deputies, Supervisors, and Administrative personnel in addition to Court Security Officers). This District was known as the "Rocket Docket" as they were very no-nonsense and cases moved swiftly through the court system.

The Alexandria Division was by far the busiest in Eastern Virginia because of its proximity to Washington, DC. Numerous international espionage trials were held in Alexandria, including Ronald Humphrey and David Truong, John Walker, Larry WU-TAI Chin, and Aldrich Ames.

A major dilemma Alexandria had was serving warrants because of jurisdictional problems after tickets were issued for parking violations at several federal properties, including National Airport, Dulles

International Airport, and the Pentagon. After tickets were issued by the Airport Police and/or Federal Protective Service, if the tickets were not adjudicated, warrants were issued, and the Marshals called in. Twenty-five thousand tickets were issued annually at the Pentagon, which had a parking capacity of ten thousand. To address the problem at the Pentagon, I put an ad in the Pentagon Monthly Newsletter indicating that arrests would be made if tickets were not paid or adjudicated by the court. Nearly 4,000 tickets were ignored by the violators, so warrants were issued. On June 29, 1978, my office parked a prison transport bus at the Pentagon's central court where Marshals arrested 28 randomly selected offenders, including a Navy Captain and a Lieutenant Colonel in the Air Force. They were taken directly to a U.S. Magistrate for adjudication, where all fines were tripled, and 90-day jail sentences were given, with jail time suspended on good behavior.

US Marshal Appointment signed by President Ronald Reagan

When U.S. Marshal Ike Hylton retired in 1986, I was appointed by the court as the United States Marshal for the Eastern District of Virginia (ED/VA). I served as United States Marshal for the ED/VA until a presidential appointment was made, at which time I was transferred to Washington, D.C., as the Senior Chief Deputy in the District of Columbia. I served in this capacity for two years before transferring back to the ED/VA as Chief Deputy.

The court then appointed me again as the United States Marshal until my Presidential nomination as US Marshal for the ED/VA was confirmed by the U.S. Senate. Having the distinct honor of receiving nominations from not one but two U.S. Presidents (Ronald Reagan and George Bush) and confirmation from the U.S. Senate, I proudly served as US Marshal for the ED/VA for close to 14 years. U.S. Presidents select Marshals based on Senate recommendation, and often, the nominee was not a career US Marshal employee. I was one of the few Marshals nominated and appointed based on merit within the US Marshals Service. I served as US Marshal until President Clinton replaced me with VA State Trooper John Marshall, the son of Supreme Court Justice Thurgood. I left the ED/VA office, transferring to the U.S. Marshals Service Headquarters, where I later retired after a very rewarding 25-year career.

U.S. Marshals
Dust Off Dodge City Image

By Jean Lionsdale Geddes

Although many people still think of a U.S. Marshal in terms of Bat Masterson or Matt Dillon, nothing could be further from the truth.

The U.S. Marshal of today is no latter-day gunslinging do-gooder, as portrayed in old westerns, but one of the most sophisticated, versatile law enforcement officers in the nation.

There are currently 94 U.S. Marshals in the country, and 2,500 employees in their service, working under the auspices of the United States Department of Justice. Their responsibilities include tracking down federal criminals, protecting people involved in court action be they judges, attorneys or witnesses, enforcing court orders, and seizing and managing assets acquired from profits of specific criminal activities.

The United States Marshal Service, the oldest law enforcement agency in the country, began in 1789 when George Washington appointed the first 13 marshals. Edward Carrington, of Culpeper, was a Virginia lawyer, a delegate to the Continental Congress and a plantation owner when he volunteered his services to the president and was named among the first of this elite group of officers.

Roger Ray, U.S. Marshal for the Eastern District of Virginia, said, "I guess you could call us generalists in the law enforcement field. We can do just about everything from structured law enforcement work to dealing with terrorist hostage situations. We are on call to the attorney general's office at all times and we can act and command whatever is necessary."

Just days after his appointment to the service in 1985, Ray was called into action with involvement in one of Northern Virginia's most sensational and talked about criminal cases to date.

He was among 100 law enforcement officers who, in January, 1985, year, seized Shelburne Glebe, a 1,000-acre Loudoun County farm near Leesburg, and arrested the owner, Christopher Reckmeyer and his brother, Robert, for directing a decade-long drug operation. Today both men are serving 16-year sentences at a federal prison in Danbury, Conn.

The undercover drug operation, dubbed "Operation Flying Carpet" because the brothers were purportedly dealing in Oriental rugs, revealed profits in excess of $100 million from the sale of hashish and marijuana. The farm was indeed stocked with Oriental carpets plus African emeralds, gold and silver and other precious gems and $200,000 in cash.

Ray was responsible for overseeing confiscated property in the name of the Government of the United States. The historic house (once the home of George Washington's chap-

ABOVE: George Washington appointing the first U.S. Marshals.
LEFT: Roger Ray, U.S. Marshal in the Eastern District of Virginia, helped nab Rick and Robert Reckmeyer for operating a drug ring from their Loudoun County farm.

lain) and land, valued at mure than $2.8 million will be sold at auction early this summer.

In the meantime, the government has paid $77,000 in fees to keep up the farm and its animals and to sdvertise its sale.

Ray said the seizure of the property was a combined efion on the part of Northem Virginia law enforcement agencies, the DEA, the U.S. Marshal Service and the F.B.I. "We had warrants based on indicaments for the anests we made. The entire operation was highly successful and efficient," he said.

Ray credlis the sophisticated capabllities of the U.S. Marshal Service, and its duration, with excellent training and field esperionce. He competed successfully in a mtional internabip program to produce qualliy management for field operstions and, in 1977, was among fhe men selected for intensive training in all phases of the Marshal Service on national and local fovels. He was appointed officially by President Reagan on Febnzary 26, 1996 for a four yesr term oversscing one of the most active dsitricts in the nation.

Prequlsties for such an appointment require rigorous traliting physical fltness and administrative and leadenhip abilitles. The U.S. Marshal Service apprehends tivo thiðls of fesleral fugitives and executes more arrest warrants than all other federal law enforcement agencies, It is aho primarily responsible for the extrodition of fugitives apprehended in foreign countries wanted for prosecution in the United Sertes.

Working through a cooperative Fugitive Investiglziive Snike Team (FIST) in conjunction with local, state and foreign laus enforcement agencies, the service has successfully apprehenden thousands of folons. During the past four years, 14,770 arrests of fugitives have been mate.

In a recent speech to the U.S. Marshal Service, President Reagan lauded it's 197-yeaa history. "You've kept your honorable traditions, but today you're fulliling your responsibilities with modern skills, technology and innovative thinking. Virtually every festeral enforcement initiative involves the Marshal Service. This all adds up to a hesvy burden of responsibillty."

It is the 94 U.S. Marshals and a team of deputtes and support personnel numbering 2,500 working with U.S. Marshal Service Director Scanley E. Morris who cany this "heary burden of responsibillty" along with a proud tradition of law enforcement which is considered by many as the nation's finest.

PHOTOGRAPH Courtesy of tise U.S. Mantal Service

Edward Carrington, of Culpeper, was among the first 13 U.S. Marshals appointed by George Washington in 1789.

Nova scope article

60

Roger and Debbie's Wedding April 24, 1982

Having never experienced "family" life, I always feared rejection and abandonment, but after eight years of dating, I asked Debbie to marry me, and she said yes! (No Redskins tickets included.) The wedding date was set for April 24, 1982, in Mitchellville, MD. Sadly, Debbie's sister, Linda (age 30) died suddenly from a heart ailment just 6 weeks before the wedding. Grief-stricken, we prayed for God's guidance during that heartbreaking time, and he led us to the altar where Debbie and I wed, surrounded by friends and our small families, feeling Linda smiling over us.

Forty Years Later, I Find My Mother

In 1988, while visiting the home, one of the people who had worked there for years gave my wife Debbie a letter that she explained might help me find my mother. Over the years, I had tried many ways to find my mother and/or dad, always being unsuccessful, as there were very few leads to follow. When Debbie told me about the letter given to her during our visit, I told her to throw it in the trash because I had looked for so many years and had gone down so many rabbit holes with leads provided by friends and acquaintances. The following year, when we visited the home, Ella (who worked at the Home for several years) was curious about why we had not followed up on the letter she had provided. I told her that I thought it was probably another false lead and that I didn't want to waste my time on it.

During our visit in April 1989, Gertrude looked good, even though she was very frustrated with Kentucky State administrators in dealing with children under her charge. At this time, there were ten children at the home, ages six to sixteen. We had a nice visit with Gertrude as well as the children. We played volleyball, brought bags of clothing and candy, and threw a pizza party for them one evening. The next day, while visiting, Ella asked us to look at some scrapbooks and gave us pictures, newspaper articles, and a letter received from Miss Lindsay dated 2/12/88. Miss Lindsay believed her sister Nettie was the mother of two children from the Ramey Home. She had a letter of agreement dated September 17, 1949, between Nettie Oney and the Ramey Home. The agreement listed two children: a girl aged two named Linda Sue Ford and a boy named Ronald Lee. She had a birth certificate for Linda Sue Ford, born August 12, 1947, to Nettie Oney and Albert Ford. However, she did not have a birth certificate for the boy.

On April 28, 1989, at my request (partly because I was both skeptical and nervous), my wife, Debbie, called Edith Lindsay. Ms. Lindsay said that she did have the agreement and a birth certificate. She explained that the welfare department had taken the children from Nettie and placed them with Gertrude. Nettie always held out hope that she could get her children back and, therefore, never agreed to allow the children to be adopted. She said that Linda was born in Greenup County. She was unsure where the boy was born, and she did say that they had different fathers.

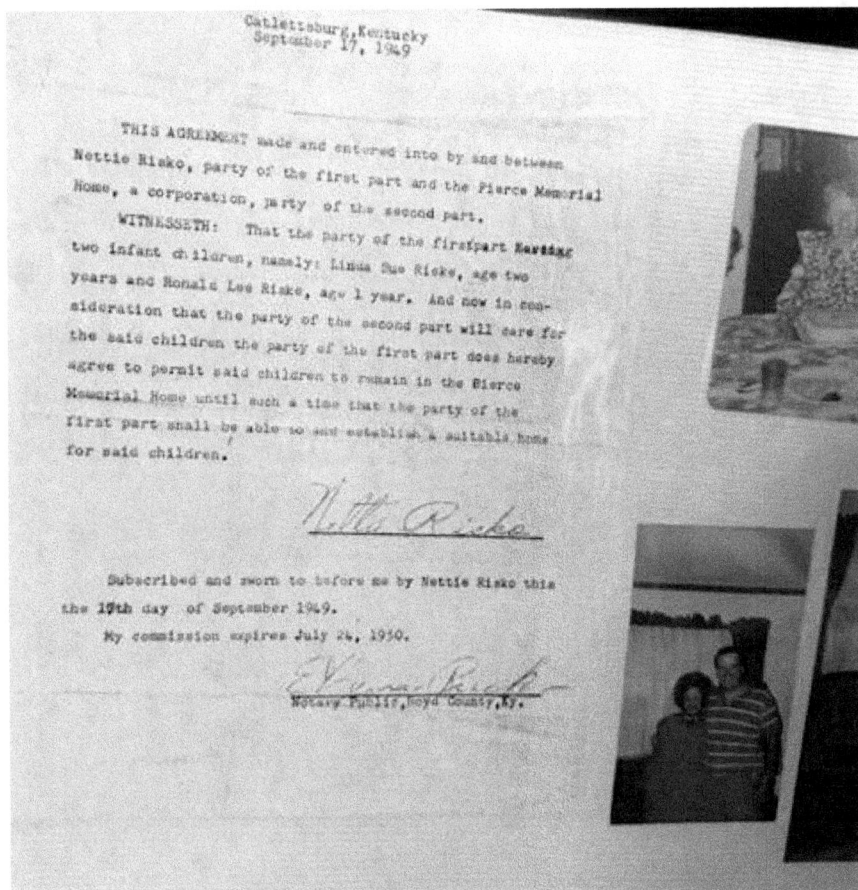

1949 Agreement Signed by Nettie Risko

Edith Lindsay indicated that Nettie had three other children. One was a Marine, and the last she heard from him, he was living in

Arkansas. She noted that she and Nettie had another sister who had passed away. She described Nettie as having long, thick, dark hair and dark eyes.

With the information provided by Edith Lindsay, I requested a Birth Records Check through the Kentucky Department of Vital Statistics and was told the search would take three to four weeks. The following name searches were requested: Ronald Lee Ford, Ronald and Roger Owney, Ronald and Roger Russo, Ronald and Roger Risko, and Roger Ford.

Roger's Birth Certificate

On May 8, 1989, we visited the Ramey Home and spoke to Ella regarding the letter from Miss Lindsay to see if she could provide any more insight. Ella said she had contacted Miss Lindsay through Shirley Cleary, the sister of Virginia "Bootsie" Baldridge. Bootsie was married to Nettie's cousin (Clyde Baldridge). Shirley had been a friend for many years, and one day, Shirley, Bootsie, and Ella were looking at photographs of some of the Ramey children. Bootsie remarked about what a resemblance there was between a boy and a girl in the pictures and her own children, saying she knew two of her husband's cousins' children were raised at the home and felt it was these two.

Shirley said that as far as she knew, Nettie lived in California and had eight to nine children, with Lindsay raising at least one of them. Also, there was a great aunt, Molly Baldridge, who resided in a nursing home in Vanceburg, Kentucky.

Conversation and correspondence notes between Roger and Bootsie (April -May 1989)

Shortly thereafter, I found Bootsie Baldridge, who was very encouraging and said that Edith Lindsay and others in the family had been hopeful that the family could all get together again. They have had reunions in the past and have always hoped they could locate all the children.

Bootsie went on to say she visited Ella's home several years ago and, while looking through scrapbooks, commented on the striking resemblance of the two children to her own. She has two children—a girl named Linda, who is a beautician, and a son named Larry. She and her husband have been married for over forty years, so she's familiar with Nettie and the family.

She said that Nettie was married to Elbert Ford but was not living with him at the time she gave birth to Linda. She was staying in her sister-in-law's home, and no one even knew she was pregnant. She went to use the outdoor toilet, and when she returned, she said someone needed to take her to the hospital so she could have her baby.

65

Bootsie believes Linda was born at either King's Daughter or Bellefonte Hospitals in Ashland, Kentucky.

She did not believe the little boy was fathered by Ford, as Nettie was no longer with him. It is uncertain if she was divorced from him at the time. It has never been confirmed, but the family believes the father of the baby boy is Carl Lake because he was going with Nettie at the time. Carl now resides in Columbus, Ohio. He is described as six-foot-two, with very broad shoulders and a wonderful personality. He is married and may not even be aware that he is the father. The last time Bootsie saw Carl was at a funeral several years ago.

Bootsie indicated that Nettie had three other children while in Kentucky—a boy named James Elmore Ford, who was nine years older than Linda/Roger and was adopted by a minister, growing up in Grundy, Virginia; a sister who married at sixteen or seventeen years old and lives in Arkansas; and another sister who Miss Edith Lindsay, your aunt, adopted.

She said Nettie had led a rough life, being raised as an orphan herself. She was married at a very young age, which led to a divorce, and she had no job. Linda was two years old, and Roger was six months to a year old. Nettie was living with friends on a houseboat on the Ohio River. She left her two young children with her friends while she went to Michigan seeking work, after which she planned to return to Kentucky and regain custody of her children. After several weeks, when she still had not returned, the friends turned the children over to the authorities.

Nettie always wanted the children to be returned and visited when they were very young. Apparently, as they grew older, Gertrude denied Nettie access to the children. Nettie would never consent to their adoption, even though there were interested parties, and she apparently held out hope she would regain custody. When we asked Miss Lindsay why she had the agreement and certificate, she said Nettie moved around quite a bit, and she wanted them kept in a secure environment. She felt it best to leave them with her sister Edith.

The grandparents were Lee Oney, who died of tuberculosis, and his wife, Mary Oney, who died of blood poisoning. Their farm was sold several years ago, and Mary's remains were removed from there to the cemetery on the hill to accommodate a strip mine. Edith handled the arrangements. Nettie and Edith's other sister was Mary Ethel, who died in an automobile accident.

Bootsie indicated it had been approximately twenty-three years since she last saw Nettie. The last she heard, Nettie was living in Anaheim, California, with her husband. He was in the Navy, and she worked in a pancake house near Disneyland. She had two more children, a boy and a girl, who are now approximately twenty-nine and thirty years old.

Bootsie said she was going to send pictures of her children so we could see the resemblance. She thinks she also has at least one picture of Nettie. She is trying to locate Nettie's phone number. Now, we "wait and see." We are awaiting Edith Lindsay's call, Bootsie's pictures, and the birth certificates from Kentucky.

The next day, Bootsie called to tell us she had found the pictures of Nettie's family and was sending them to us, along with photos of her children. She also wrote a note with names and additional information. Roger spoke with Bootsie and her husband, Clyde, for about forty-five minutes as they related the following: the Oney family is a mix of English, Irish, and hillbilly ancestry. Their religion is Protestant and Baptist. The Oney farm was located about ten minutes from Ashland in Greenup County, consisting of approximately one hundred acres, filled with walnut and poplar trees, and was sold for strip mining.

Debbie was making all of the calls to these various sources because I continued thinking it was a waste of time. When Debbie told me that Bootsie indicated that Diane, Nettie's daughter, whom Edith adopted, was the one who was called "Miss Dallas," I thought that was interesting. In addition, she said Diane was a Dallas Cowboys cheerleader and was born in 1950, which is two years younger than me. I thought this was either very comical or coincidental, as Debbie was a Washington Redskins cheerleader for eight years. Subsequently, I found out that Diane was not a Dallas Cowboys cheerleader but rather a majorette at the University of Texas, where she went to college and became a schoolteacher. Tales have a way of growing in the South – bless their hearts!

Debbie phoned Edith Lindsay on May 10, 1989. Edith read the letter of agreement between Nettie Risco and the Pierce Memorial Children's Home, also known as the Gertrude Ramey Children's Home. The agreement stated that two infant children, Linda Sue Riske, age two, and Ronald Lee Riske, age one, would remain at the home until she was able to establish herself and care for them. The agreement was dated September 17, 1949, and signed by Nettie Risko (apparently, legalities such as proper name spellings were overlooked). Miss Lindsay did not know the origin of the name "Risko." She said the birth certificate for Linda shows that Nettie was twenty-eight when she had her. The birth certificate appears to be quite difficult to read. Edith read that Nettie had eight children before Linda; she couldn't account for them, but knew of two other children—James Elmore Ford, born in 1941, and Luna Mae, born January 8, 1935. Diane, who was born in 1950, was adopted by Edith. She has two children, Crystal and Lindsay Dyer. Diane lives in Fort Worth, Texas. The Lindsays' other child is James Edward Lindsay, who lives in Dallas, Texas. Miss Lindsay said she would try to reach Nettie once we were certain she was our mother.

Roger explained how he was called "Risko" when he was young and that he and Linda were the only children at the home of the proper ages. At that time, he was the only boy there. Edith also said she would send us a copy of the birth certificate and the letter of agreement. Though we don't have many, we are sending her pictures of Linda and Roger when they were very young.

Debbie put together a package of pictures and newspaper articles of Linda and Roger when they were little for Edith. When she called Edith to inform her that the package was on its way, I told Debbie to ask Edith what kind of medical condition I had when I arrived at the

68

Ramey Home. If she could answer that question, it would confirm that Nettie was my mother. Edith said she did not know of any medical condition Roger may have had, but assured Debbie that she would ask Nettie that question when they talked.

Nettie disclosed to Edith that Roger had a hernia, but did not have the resources to have it corrected at the hospital. After hearing this information, I had no doubt that Nettie Heidner was my mother. Nettie asked Edith to pass her phone number and current address in El Dorado, California, to Roger. When the reality hit me that I finally knew who my mother was, I was totally overwhelmed with emotion, feelings I had never experienced before. This was the woman who gave me birth, the one I had searched for years and years to find. I was in total shock because all the pieces fell into place so easily once we pursued the leads.

If Debbie, my wife, had not been persistent in following these leads, I would have never found my mother. I will always be eternally grateful for that persistence. Again, God works in mysterious ways, and I know this would not have happened without God continuing to watch over me in my life journey.

On May 12, 1989, when I was forty years old, I called my mother for the very first time in my life. I didn't ask any questions; I just reiterated how happy I was to have found her. She said she had always loved Linda and me and never gave up hope of reuniting with us. She apologized for not being able to care for us and said she had visited the Ramey Home several times, but the staff kept giving her reasons why she couldn't see her children.

She mentioned that she had lived in California for about twenty-five years. She divorced Mr. Heidner in 1970. She has two children: Gloria, who is about 35 years old, and is separated from her husband. Gloria has two children and is pregnant with her third. She lives in California near Nettie. Nettie also has a son, Eddie, who is 37 and lives with her. Eddie is divorced and has custody of his children; he was disabled by a car accident that left him with an artificial hip. Nettie has heart problems and takes nitroglycerin tablets, but is generally in good shape.

She is seventy years old, born on November 18, 1919. She said she has owned several businesses over the years and worked as a florist for a while. I told her I would love to fly her to Washington so she, Linda, and I could meet. She was very excited about the idea. I plan to stay in touch to figure out when she can visit.

After our conversation that night, I immediately called a florist and ordered her a dozen red roses for Mother's Day. It was one of the best feelings I've ever had. Finally, I had a reason to celebrate Mother's Day!

Nettie Comes to Washington

Linda and I convinced our mother that it would be a great reunion if she would visit my home in Northern Virginia. She agreed to come, and Debbie made travel arrangements for her to fly from Sacramento, California, to Dulles Airport in Virginia. On the day she was to arrive, I was very nervous, waiting for the time to pick up this woman who was believed to be my birth Mom. It sounds strange even as I write about the events leading up to and the emotions of finally setting eyes on my birth Mother. Debbie, Linda, and I agreed that only Linda and I would meet Nettie at the airport. In my recently purchased Buick Riviera, I drove Linda and myself to Dulles Airport. The anticipation of meeting my mother for the first time was both frightening and euphoric.

After arriving at Dulles Airport, Linda and I proceeded to the terminal where Nettie was arriving on time. Linda and I stood there with the few pictures we had of Nettie, trying to decipher which arriving passenger was her. Passengers were picking up their bags and leaving, and we still had not spotted anyone we believed could be our mother. With the terminal almost empty, we finally saw a petite woman in a short black dress, black fishnet-like stockings, a white blouse, and high heels, looking very lost. We approached her and asked if she was Nettie, and she replied that she was. To say that we were surprised at her attire would be an understatement! After embracing, we gathered her bags from baggage claim and proceeded to my car while enjoying small talk about her trip and what she would like to do while in the Washington, D.C., area.

Once in the car, Linda got into the back seat, Nettie got into the front passenger seat, and I drove to our home in Vienna, Virginia. On the drive home, Nettie pulled out a cigarette and was about to light it when Linda advised her that I did not allow smoking in my car. Nettie did not light the cigarette, and we proceeded to my home in Vienna, Virginia. When we arrived, Debbie greeted Nettie with a hug and invited her into our home. We were all nervous and asked Nettie if she would like anything, to which she replied a "Rusty Nail." I had never heard of a Rusty Nail cocktail, but Nettie told us what the ingredients were. Debbie made the drink with one and a half ounces of bourbon, three-quarters of an ounce of Drambuie, a lemon twist, and ice.

We enjoyed Nettie's company and small talk, but it was obvious she was very tired. I asked if she wanted to go to bed, and she responded that it would be very nice. We told Nettie that we were having a few friends over the next day to meet her poolside at our home. The next day, the pool party was to begin at 1 p.m. At 1:00, Nettie was still sleeping, and while we didn't want to disturb her, Linda got worried or perhaps impatient and suggested that we should go in and check on her. Around 4 p.m., Linda and Debbie went to Nettie's room, and Linda used a small mirror to place under Nettie's nose to ensure she was still breathing, which caused Nettie to wake up. She apologized for sleeping so late and said she would be joining the party shortly.

When she finally came down and joined us outside with a few remaining guests, she asked for another Rusty Nail. Debbie made her one, and I can honestly say I was both amused and amazed that I was in the presence of my birth mother after all these years. I always addressed her as Nettie, while Linda constantly called her "Mother" and put her on the spot with questions that, in my opinion, were not easy for Nettie to answer at that time. It was while listening to Nettie, I learned that she had given birth to 7 or 8 children and traveled across the country trying to find work and a home to care for her children. She did not provide answers to our abandonment, nor her desire to reunite with us when we were children. It was obvious to me from my conversations with Nettie that some of the truth and evidence I had uncovered once I discovered her identity were not always accurate or complete.

Nettie was very petite, had a great smile, and seemed pleased with her surroundings, knowing that two of her children had done well. We enjoyed her company and her stories about her upbringing and the family she had now. She had two adult children (Eddie and Gloria) living with her. Nettie was very kind and really tried to make us feel as comfortable as possible under circumstances that were hard to explain.

We treated her with great respect because of her willingness to visit and provide answers to any questions we might have. She must have been under great pressure to sit there with Linda and me, knowing that she had abandoned us decades earlier. She blamed the Ramey Home and Gertrude for her having to move on in life without us because Gertrude would not give us back to her. Though I was skeptical of what really transpired, what mattered at that visit was that we were able to reunite after all these years and have real conversations with my birth mother.

I knew that she had a tough life and had probably always done the best she could, but I still wonder, even today, what it would've been like to have been raised by her. My birth certificate lists my name as Ronald Lee Lake, with my father's name as Carl Lake. I asked Nettie about Carl Lake, and she told me that she did not know a Carl Lake. I had already discovered that the Lake family and my mother and her two sisters were neighbors. Her sister Mary, who had died in a car accident years earlier, had been married to one of the Lake brothers. My mother insisted that Carl Lake was not my father.

She showed me a picture of herself with a man whom she claimed was my birth father, though she thought his last name was Risko.

Nettie Oney and Mr. Risko

Nettie's 1ˢᵗ Visit to Roger's home in Virginia

She continued to assure me that Carl Lake was not my father. I found Carl Lake through my research into the Lake family. When I talked to him, he was totally surprised by the questions and the possibility of being my father. He told me that he had dated Nettie for some time and admitted that, yes, he might have been my dad. I did not confront my mother with this information. Still, I thought it would be worthwhile to arrange a reunion of my mother's family (the

Oney's) and possibly my father's family (the Lakes) at Greenbo Lake in eastern Kentucky at a future date.

Debbie and I invited Nettie to come back and visit with us, and we would make arrangements to have a family reunion with friends and neighbors from her past. She agreed, and so we began making plans to fly her back to Virginia and return to Kentucky for the reunion.

Roger, Nettie, and Debbie in the ED/VA US Marshal's Office

Hidden in Plain Sight

In April 1990, Debbie and I invited all the Oneys and Lakes to an Oney Reunion at Greenbo Lake. We met many cousins and others who were related to the Oney family in one way or another. One individual stands out in my mind because she was known as the matriarch of the family, Mollie Baldridge, who was 85 years old. Linda and I introduced ourselves to Miss Baldridge, and she chastised us for not staying in contact with the family. We didn't have a long conversation, but Linda and I both agreed that it felt as if we had been deserted by family rather than having been left at the Ramey Children's Home due to circumstances beyond our control. It felt like we had been hidden in plain sight.

The biggest surprise of the reunion came when I discovered that my school bus driver was a distant cousin who had transported me to and from school for several years. Everyone was very friendly, and I truly enjoyed their company. We were able to visit the hundred-plus acres that the Oneys had previously owned. Nettie was very pleased to see family and friends she had not seen in many years. The trip to her homestead, where she was raised, brought tears to her eyes. Debbie and I were grateful to have been able to give her this gift, reminding her of her childhood in Greenup County, particularly the memories she shared with her sister Edith.

Debbie, Nettie, and I returned to Virginia. After reminiscing about the people we met and spoke to at the reunion, I prepared for her to return to California to be with her family. We invited Nettie to a third visit over Thanksgiving at my sister Linda Ray Huddleson's home in Dayton, Ohio. She accepted our invitation, and as we said goodbye, we were grateful this goodbye wouldn't last decades, but God willing, we'd be together in just a few short months.

The week of Thanksgiving arrived, and Debbie and I drove to my sister's house in Dayton, Ohio, to share the holiday with Nettie. To our surprise, my cousin Clyde Baldridge and his wife, "Bootsie," also accepted Linda's invitation to join us for Thanksgiving. Bootsie and Clyde Baldridge were wonderful company and shared stories about the old days in Kentucky. They talked so much about people that I couldn't remember all the names, who they were, or how they were related to me, but it was enlightening to hear. Clyde, my brother-in-law Jerry and and I went on Wednesday evening to pick up Nettie. Greeting Nettie at the Dayton airport, I did not feel the same anxiety I had felt back in Virginia when I met her for the first time.

We had a wonderful Thanksgiving and enjoyed time with my nieces and nephews, my birth mother, and my cousins. Before Nettie left on Saturday, she had one request: she asked that Debbie and I consider adopting the grandchild she brought from California (Eddie's daughter). Eddie had been in a bad accident and was not able to care for her, and Nettie thought it best that she be given up for adoption. We were startled at that request – to say the least –but said no. That being said……. It was one of the best Thanksgivings I could have had with my birth Mother.

My sister asked me why I didn't call Nettie "Mom," since she was calling her that. I told my sister that yes, she was my birth mother, but I still hadn't confirmed whether I was a Ray, Lake, or Risco/Risko. Any questions about why we were abandoned at the Ramey Home, or why she never returned or inquired about us or our well-being, were never answered.

I told Linda that I had found peace of mind in finding my birth mother and trying to piece together who my dad was—or wasn't. I told her I did not harbor any deep feelings for my birth mother other than being thankful for my life. I have seen enough to know that I have not had the worst life. I came to realize that I was blessed in many ways growing up. I always had a roof over my head, food on the table, and a good understanding of what was right and wrong. I was required to go to church and was taught early on that Jesus loved me. When things were tough and I needed to overcome circumstances beyond my control, Jesus was always there for me.

I also continued to talk to Carl Lake from time to time, and he believed that he was my father. I have never fully convinced myself of this because of conflicting stories and the timing of my birth.

This was a fascinating time in my life. While regretting that forty years had passed before we met, I believe that my maturity and financial stability helped soften the shock. I can't imagine how an impressionable twenty-year-old would have reacted. I am grateful that I was able to meet the man and woman listed on what I believe to be my real birth certificate, though I wish I had met them earlier to learn more about them and, frankly, my genetics. Because of the lost decades and Nettie and Carl's advanced ages, our time getting to know each other was very short-lived. Carl Lake passed away in March 1988, at which time his daughters made it obvious they wanted no further contact with me. I respected their wishes and have not spoken to the Lakes since. Gertrude Ramey died on April 5, 2009. Me, my sister Linda, my wife Debbie, and numerous others attended her funeral and burial. Preceding her death, we attended several Ramey Home reunions. Nettie passed away in February 1992. I was notified of her passing by her son, Eddie, who enlisted my help with her burial expenses. Because she was my birth Mother and felt she deserved a proper burial, I obliged with the request.

Son finds mother after 40 years

WASHINGTON (AP) — U.S. Marshall Roger Ray, reared in an Ashland, Ky., orphanage, solved his toughest case when he found his mother after a 40 year separation.

Their first reunion took place by telephone last May. "It was the Friday before Mother's Day," Ray said.

"I was shaking all over because I was so scared. I just told her who I was and that I thought I was her son."

Nettie Heidner, identified on Ray's birth certificate as Nettie Oney, said she trembled a little herself. "I figured God had done me the biggest favor of the world," she told the Washington Post recently.

Ms. Heidner, now 71 and living outside Sacramento, Calif., said she was impressed with the accomplishments of her son, a 19-year member of the U.S. Marshals Service. He began by driving defendants from the District of Columbia Jail to Superior Court and now oversees the entire Eastern District of Virginia.

Ray was separated from his mother in 1949, a few weeks short of his first birthday. As Ms. Heidner tells it, she left Roger and his 2-year-old sister, Linda, with a babysitter while she worked at a hotel near their home in Ashland.

The babysitter let children run loose and police, responding to neighborhood complaints, took them to an orphanage later known as the Ramey Children's Home.

Ms. Heidner said that when she attempted to pick up her children, a judge told her to come back when she could provide something better than the one-room house where they lived.

Turn to SON, Page 9

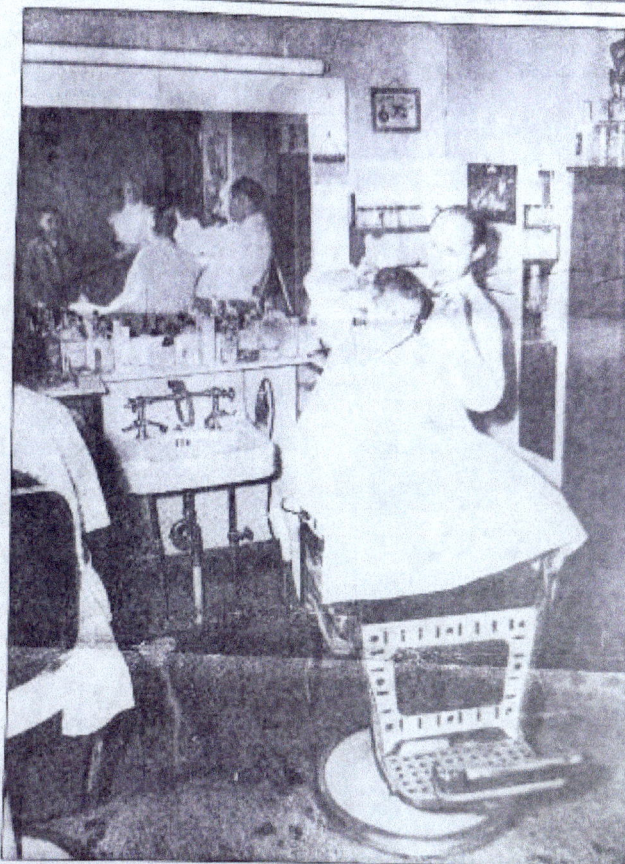

The late John W. Todd Sr. cuts Roger Ray's hair when he was about four or five years old in this photo taken in the mid 1950s. Ray said Todd befriended him and would slip him a quarter "every now and then."

But he'll always call Gertrude Ramey 'mom'

By JIM TODD
Senior News Writer

ASHLAND — Roger Ray is 99.9 percent sure that Nettie Heidner of Sacramento, Calif., is the mother who gave birth to him and who he didn't see for nearly 40 years until last May.

Ray is 100 percent sure that Gertrude Ramey is the mother who gave him the love, caring and inner strength to make a success out of his life and who he will always call "mom."

Ray, 41, a U.S. Marshal who oversees the Eastern District of Virginia, and his sister, Linda Lou Ray-Huddleston of Dayton, Ohio, were reared in the Gertrude Ramey Children's Home here after their biological mother could not afford to take care of them.

On Sept. 14, 1949, The Independent ran a picture of Roger and Linda with a caption that read:

"The two babies, pictured above, believed to have been abandoned by their mother, were admitted to the Pierce Memorial Children's Home

later changed to the Gertrude Ramey Children's Home) here yesterday afternoon. Miss Gertrude Ramey, director of the home, said County Judge E.K. Rose had the babies placed in the home. Juvenile authorities found the youngsters in the residence of Ruby McConnell, 3201 Croshy St., who said the mother had left them about 10 days ago and did not return. She did not remember the name of the mother. The girl baby, at the left, is believed to be about 22 months of age, and the boy baby about 10 months old."

Although there are varying accounts about how and why the two youngsters ended up at the Ramey Home, Ray says that's not the most important thing to him now.

"I just wanted to find out who my mother was," he said in a telephone interview Friday. "That's the reason I elected to find her. I told Gertrude that this woman may be my biological mother, but that she is 'mom' to me."

Turn to BUT, Page 9

ing to Bob McCullough Drive off U.S. 60, dogs the children would claim usually ended up getting hit by cars on Winchester, Ramey said.

After some Armco Steel Co. employees built a fence around the property, Ramey got a collie for the children. Roger named the dog Armco and claimed it for his own, Ramey remembers.

"Roger trained Armco to open the ice box," she said with a laugh. "Armco slept with him and kept him from going out into the street. I would tell Armco not to let Roger go over the fence and that dog would get hold of his pants and not let go of him."

When reminded of the story, Ray laughed and said it was all true.

Ramey said Linda was a beautiful girl who was extremely artistic and loved music.

"Now she's one of the wisest and best mothers I have ever seen," Ramey said. "She has two children and a grandchild now and she visits

about every other month. She's a beautician and cuts the boys' hair when she visits."

The home currently is home to 20 teen-age boys.

Ramey said one of her favorite stories about Roger is when he and three other children from the home accompanied her in 1959 to have dinner with Eleanor Roosevelt at her New York apartment, and later to the White House during the Eisenhower Administration.

"Miss Roosevelt was talking about a trip to Russia, and Roger, who was 10, asked, 'Mrs. Roosevelt, just what are the conditions in Russia?'

"Miss Roosevelt said, 'I predict that you'll be a future president.'

"Then when we got to Washington, we went into the Oval Office and Roger sat in the president's chair," Ramey said.

"I said, 'Roger!'

"And he said, 'If I'm going to be a future president I have to see what it feels like — and I'm tired.'"

Son finds

Continued from Page 1

Returning to the orphanage later, Ms. Heidner said she was informed that her son and daughter had been adopted. Needing work, she left Kentucky for the promise of better jobs in Michigan and later in California.

Kentucky court records identify Carl Lake of Columbus, Ohio, as the father of Ronald Lee Lake, also known during his childhood by other names, including Roger Ray.

Lake, a 68-year-old former railroad and steel factory worker, said he and Nettie dated but never married. Lake said he knew that Nettie delivered a child by him but never knew what happened to the boy.

"I don't feel real close to him in one way, but in another way I feel like he's mine," Lake said. He said Ray calls at least every other week. "I'll treat him like a son. ...I'm sorry he had to spend so much time in the home but I didn't know."

When Ray was 12, officials of the children's home decided he was old enough to be transferred to a nearby boys farm, thus separating him from his sister, his only known relative.

At 17, Ray left the farm with the clothes on his back and a used car he had purchased for $50. After sampling classes at the University of Kentucky, he enlisted in the Army. In the early 1970s, he joined the Marshals' Service in Washington and Virginia.

Then, as now, he made annual treks to the orphanage to visit old friends, treat the children to pizza and rummage through boxes of photo albums and letters.

"There wasn't anything I didn't

try to turn over to see if I could find something," Ray said. Everything was a dead end, including courthouse records.

Linda Lou Ray-Huddleston, the marshal's sister in Dayton, also searched unsuccessfully. Eventually, the two decided to give up their quest.

Two years ago, the clue that Ray needed came in a letter to the orphanage from Edith Lindsay, an aunt that he never knew he had.

Ms. Lindsay explained that Virginia Baldridge, the wife of one of Nettie Heidner's cousins, had visited the orphanage and spotted pictures of Roger and Linda in an employee's scrapbook.

The letter also said Ms. Lindsay had a birth certificate for Linda Sue Ford and an agreement in which the orphanage agreed to care for Ronald Lee. The agreement was signed by Ms. Lindsay's sister, Nettie Oney.

Ms. Lindsay asked the orphanage if the children in the picture were the same children in the documents she held.

Ray received the letter last year and contacted Ms. Lindsay, who wasn't convinced that he was her sister's son. The last piece of evidence fell in place when Ray told of the scar that he carried from an abdominal operation while he was in the orphanage.

Within weeks of Ray's telephone call to his mother, he and his sister were picking her out of a crowd at Dulles International Airport.

The two-week visit that followed went well, Ray said.

He said he had a lot of questions about the past and expected there would be answers in time. But for now, they're not important, he said.

Continued from Page 1

Finding his real mother has given Ray a "sense of purpose or belonging," he said. "It gives you a reason for being. Although there are still a lot of unanswered questions, that's not important," he said. "The most important is that we had a beginning somewhere, and that's been satisfied."

But Ray is unsure who his father is.

After he discovered his birth certificate (through an aunt two years ago,) Ray located the man listed as his father — Carl Lake of Columbus, Ohio. Linda's birth certificate listed her last name as Ford.

Lake, 68, had agreed to undergo a DNA test at Johns Hopkins Hospital in Baltimore, Md., to determine if he is Ray's dad.

"That's the only positive way to do it," Ray said. "We hope to do it this year."

Heidner says Lake is not Ray's father. She claims a man with a last name of Risko, who was in the service, is the father of both Roger and Linda.

"She said he sent her support money while she was pregnant with me, but then she found out he was already married," Ray said.

Although Heidner told Ray she did not put Lake down as her son's last name on his birth certificate, the certificate shows that she provided the information, Ray said.

What confuses Ray most is that his mother had several relatives in the area, but none of them came forward to claim relation, even after his and Linda's pictures were in the newspaper.

"I have no idea why," he said. "It's very strange."

But Ray is not remorseful about his earlier years.

"I told Linda that we're better off under the circumstances because our mother just couldn't take care of us and that we are lucky we were raised at the Ramey Home. Gertrude was our guardian angel more than anything else. And when I look at the other children (Heidner) raised (later), I think we're better off."

Ramey says Ray was an unusually intelligent little boy, who as a baby, clinged to her as a mother.

"He slept with me for about a month until he was strong enough to have an operation (for a hernia) he needed when he was brought here," she said.

"Growing up he loved to go to school," she said. "He was never absent or tardy. But he was mischievous, too — just all boy.

"I remember that he had done something I didn't want him to do when he was about eight or nine, and I told him to come inside the home and to sit in a chair. He came in, but didn't want to sit in the chair. He said, 'Gertrude, you can't punish someone twice for the same crime.'"

When the home was located at 2318 Winchester Ave., before mov-

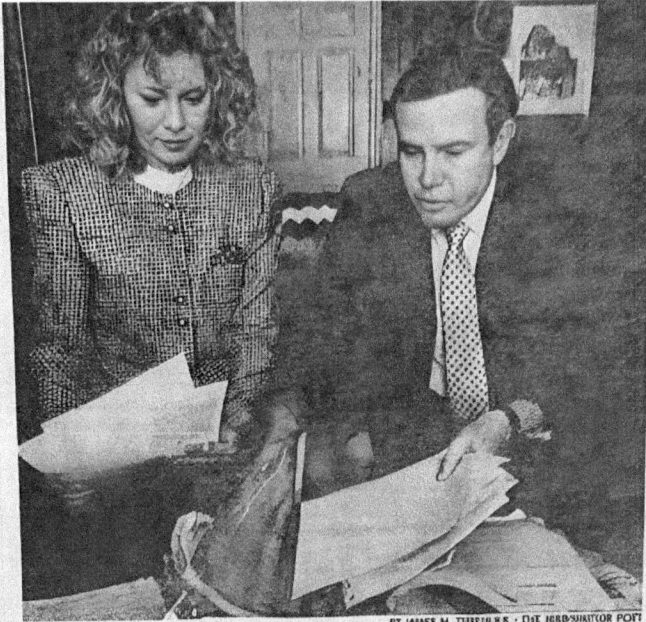

Roger Ray, of Fairfax, looks at old newspaper clippings with his wife, Debbie.

Lawman Digs Deep—and Uncovers His Roots

U.S. Marshal Raised in Orphanage Finds His Mother After Decades

By Robert F. Howe
Washington Post Staff Howe

U.S. Marshal Roger Ray finally solved his toughest case. After more than 30 years, he found his mom.

Ray, 41, has spent two decades riding herd on deng fords, thieves and jillers. Bat no felcm over numbed him with the kind of fear he folf the day be phoned his mother for the first time.

"It was the Friday before Mother's Day," said Ray, who hid lost licned his mother's voke 40 years ego, hoare betere palice placed him io an Apoalachian Kentucky orphanage. "I was ahahing all over becaunt I was so scared. I innt tuid hor wlur I was and that I thought I was ber son . . .

"I must have talked to hor for a half-hour, hat it seemed like two mientes. The whole time, I was scared that she might liang up and I would never be able to reach her agnin."

Nettie Heidner, identified on Ray's birth certificate as Nettie Onsy, and she trembled a little herself—hut with prsle and high spirits. "I figured God had done me the higgest faver of the worid." she said. Ray "sent me two doren roses, and hs said in the note what a wonderful fecling it sras to send his own mother roses for Mother's Day."

Heidner, now 71 and living ontside Sacranmnts, Calif., and she was impresced with the accomplishmeats of her son, a 10 yeat mendier of the U.S. Macahals Service who hegen by darring defendants from the U.C. Jail to Supe-

rior Court and now oversses the entire Eastern District of Virginia.

"I couhln't believe how well he'd dong," she said. "Bat I would have loved him it he hadn't been dning nothing."

Over the years, Ray, who lires in Pairfar County, has diected infernal investigations, exveufed thisssinds of criminal writs and worked in the federal witaess protection progcaes, establiahing now ideniitiea for others while, in private, seaking his own.

"He cone from nothing, and a lot of people nould tend to uae that as as eacuss to fall." and Dobtie Ray, his wife of cight years, "flut he went the other nay and used it as a motvation to succeed."

Ray was suparated from his

See MASSHAL, 87, Col. 1

81

U.S. Marshal Stays on the Case, Uncovers His Roots

MARSHAL, From B1

mother in 1949, a few weeks short of his first birthday. As Heidner tells it, she left Roger and his 2-year-old sister, Linda, with a babysitter while she worked at a modest hotel near their home in Ashland, Ky.

The babysitter let the children run loose, and local police, responding to neighborhood complaints, gathered up the children and delivered them to a local orphanage later known as the Ramey Children's Home. Heidner said that when she tried to retrieve Roger and Linda, a judge called her one-room house unfit and told her to come back when she could provide a better home.

"Roger was very sick at the time," Heidner said. "He had a very bad [abdominal] rupture, and I was trying to get enough money to get him operated on." The home arranged for Roger to have a hernia operation days after he'd been brought there.

Later, when his mother returned to the home for a visit, she was told that her children had been adopted. Heidner—who had had a tough life of her own, losing both parents before she was 10 and marrying twice by age 15—needed work. So she left Kentucky for the promise of better jobs in Michigan and, later, California.

Kentucky court records identify Carl Lake, of Columbus, Ohio, as the father of Ronald Lee Lake, also known during his childhood as Roger Ray, Roger Risko, Roger Lake, Roger Oney, Roger Russo and Roger Ford.

Lake, a 68-year-old former railroad and steel factory worker, said he and Nettie dated but never married. Lake said he knew that Nettie delivered a child by him, but didn't know what happened to the boy.

"I don't feel real close to him in one way, but in another way I feel like he's mine," said Lake, adding that Ray now calls at least every other week. "At least I'll treat him like a son . . . . I'm sorry he had to spend so much time in the home, but I didn't know."

Ray's quest began when he entered first grade.

"I have a memory of being in school and the other kids having parents and going home to them," said Ray, recalling that he blackened the eyes of the few who teased him. "But I was always going back to the home, so you realize that there's something different . . . .

"I always thought that maybe my father had been killed in the war and my mother got run over or in a car accident," he said. "You know, I would fantasize about what happened. But then you understand that a family has extensions—aunts and uncles and cousins and everything else. There should be somebody out there who knows something."

Things got worse when Ray turned 12. Ramey administrators decided that he was old enough to be transferred to a nearby boys farm, meaning he would be separated from his sister, his only known relative.

"That just absolutely destroyed me because I didn't understand it," Ray said. "It was the first time that it had happened to me, that I was moved from what I considered home—I'm being rejected, I'm being pushed out."

But when the station wagon pulled up, he bit his lip and climbed in. "You got to work with what you're dealt," he said.

Ray launched his search in earnest when he turned 17, having left the farm with the clothes on his back and a used car he had picked up for $50. While living at the Ashland YMCA, he combed through clips at the Ashland Daily Independent, which had run dozens of features about the Ramey home.

He was pictured with several of the stories, including one about a trip to New York and Washington during which Gertrude Ramey, founder of

Roger Ray's mother, Nettie Heidner, in her home outside Sacramento, Calif.

BY ASSOCIATED PRESS FOR THE WASHINGTON POST

After sampling classes at the University of Kentucky, Ray enlisted in the Army, where he served as a military policeman, and in the early '70s, he joined the Marshals Service in Washington and Virginia. Then, as now, he made annual treks to the orphanage to visit old friends, treat the children to pizza and rummage through boxes of photo albums and letters.

"There wasn't anything I didn't try to turn over to see if I could find out something," Ray said. " . . . But everything was just a complete dead stone." So were courthouse records, although his law enforcement training taught him how to check and double-check for family documents.

Linda Lou Ray-Huddleson, Ray's sister in Dayton, said she talked with hundreds of people around the area where she and her brother grew up. But nobody had heard the

name Ray. "No matter what I did, nothing helped me because I didn't know [our mother's] name," she said. "I even thought of being hypnotized to go back and see if I could remember her name."

Roger and Linda said they ultimately tried to give up on their long-lost family. "I thought, it's just not meant to be," Ray said. " . . . I sort of put it out of my mind except when I would go visit [the orphanage]—until this letter came up, and I didn't give it much weight at first."

The letter, to the Ramey home from an aunt Ray never knew he had, was the clue he needed.

Erth Lindsay wrote the letter two years ago, saying she had a birth certificate for Linda Sue Ford and an agreement in which the Ramey home agreed to care for Ronald Lee. The contract was signed by Lindsay's sister, Nettie Oney.

Lindsay addressed the letter to an orphanage employee who had received a visit two or three years earlier from Lindsay's friend, Virginia "Bootsie" Baldridge, the wife of one of Nettie's cousins. Baldridge saw photos of Roger and Linda in the employee's scrapbooks and remarked how similar they looked to her own children.

"It was like looking at my own son and daughter," Baldridge said. She promptly told Lindsay, who remembered the documents Nettie had given her for safekeeping.

"Would love to know if this is the same children," Lindsay's letter concluded. "If it is, I am their aunt."

Shortly after Ray was given the letter last year, he called Lindsay. But she was not convinced that Roger Ray was her sister's son until the last piece of evidence fell neatly into place: the abdominal rupture. Ray had the scar to prove his lineage.

Within weeks of Ray's first phone call to his mother, he and his sister were picking her out of a crowd at Dulles International Airport.

"They made pictures and pictures," Heidner said. "I said, I'm so ugly I'd rather not have no pictures.' And he said, 'You're beautiful to me.'"

Everyone said the two-week visit went well, aside from a handful of unanswered questions: Why didn't Nettie seek out the family that had supposedly adopted her children? Why didn't relatives know that Roger and Linda spent over a decade in an orphanage not two miles from their homes?

Ray said he expects answers in time, but for now, they're not important.

"She had told me what she wanted to tell me, and I didn't want to give her the third degree by saying, 'This is not so, and that's not so,' " he said. "I mean, it took me 40 years to find the lady. I just didn't want her to have a bad time . . . . I love the lady. I don't have any hard feelings."

Following my Marshal's Service retirement in 1996, I served as the Executive Director for Police, Fire, and Public Safety Officers for Bob Dole's presidential campaign.

In 1998, the Commonwealth of Virginia Supreme Court appointed me Magistrate Judge for the 20th Judicial District, where I served for seven years. A principal function of a magistrate was to provide an independent, unbiased review of a complaint of criminal conduct brought by law enforcement or the general public. Duties included issuing arrest, search, and civil warrants, summonses, emergency protective and custody orders. Magistrates also conducted bail hearings to determine if an arrested individual should be released from custody prior to trial.

Additionally, during that period, I also provided security during the George W. Bush inauguration.

July 25, 1996

Mr. Roger Ray
9802 Bridleridge Court
Vienna, Virginia 22181

Dear Roger:

Please accept my sincere thanks for becoming a member of the Police, Fire and Public Safety Officers Coalition for Dole '96.

The National Chairman of our Coalition is J. Eldon (Jerry) Yates, who served as Vice Chairman of Maryland Governor Schaefer's Executive Advisory Council with oversight of all state committees on law enforcement including: coordination of local, state, and federal law enforcement efforts in the State of Maryland. Roger Ray, Executive Director of the Coalition, served 26 years in Federal law enforcement including serving as U.S. Marshal for the Eastern District of Virginia under Presidents Ronald Reagan and George Bush. I am confident that under their leadership, the Coalition will serve to enhance the public's perception of what the Dole '96 Campaign stands for and our differences with the current Administration concerning public safety.

Chairman Yates and Executive Director Ray will be appointing State Chairmen in the very near future who shall have our full support to form state steering committees in coordination with Dole '96 state committees to get out the vote this November.

The Police, Fire and Public Safety Officers for Dole '96 Coalition has demonstrated enthusiasm, integrity, and commitment to my election in 1996. I congratulate you on becoming a member of the Coalition.

Again, please accept my thanks for all your efforts. I am positive your endeavors will ensure victory in 1996.

Sincerely,

BOB DOLE

Letter of Thanks from Bob Dole

Inaugural Committee Certificate Signed by
President George W. Bush

Twentieth Judicial Circuit Commemorative Plaque

The Ray Family

From the time we were married, Debbie and I prayed to have children but endured infertility disappointments. After several years, God answered our prayers, showing us that "adoption is an option" when he brought a beautiful little girl into our lives. Our daughter Caitlin was born in 1992, and in 1996, we adopted once more when our son Christopher was born. Both Caitlin and Chris had much talent in their own ways – Caitlin loved music, acting, and horseback riding, while Chris was artistic, creative, and a talented left-handed pitcher during his middle and high school years. From the moment we laid eyes on our beautiful day-old babies, we have been grateful that God entrusted their care to us.

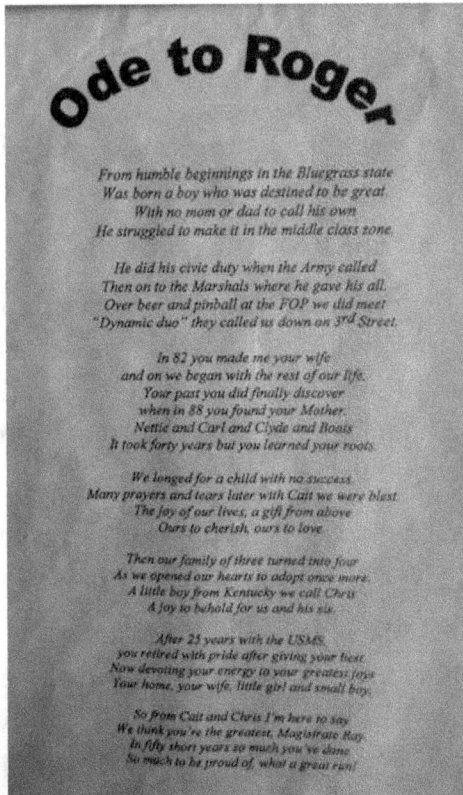

Ode to Roger

From humble beginnings in the Bluegrass state
Was born a boy who was destined to be great.
With no mom or dad to call his own
He struggled to make it in the middle class zone.

He did his civic duty when the Army called
Then on to the Marshals where he gave his all.
Over beer and pinball at the FOP we did meet
"Dynamic duo" they called us down on 3rd Street.

In 82 you made me your wife
and on we began with the rest of our life.
Your past you did finally discover
when in 88 you found your Mother.
Nettie and Carl and Clyde and Boots
It took forty years but you learned your roots.

We longed for a child with no success.
Many prayers and tears later with Cait we were blest.
The joy of our lives, a gift from above
Ours to cherish, ours to love.

Then our family of three turned into four
As we opened our hearts to adopt once more.
A little boy from Kentucky we call Chris
A joy to behold for us and his sis.

After 25 years with the USMS,
you retired with pride after giving your best.
Now devoting your energy to your greatest joys
Your home, your wife, little girl and small boy.

So from Cait and Chris I'm here to say
We think you're the greatest, Magistrate Ray.
In fifty short years so much you've done
So much to be proud of, what a great run!

50th Birthday Poem written by Debbie

87

Family memories of birthday celebrations, holiday gatherings, and vacations, which most people experience, were non-existent for me. I never had the benefit of learning parenting skills from my Mother or Father, but truly strived to be present and supportive during Caitlin and Chris' formative years, and create family memories for them.

They say "life comes full circle," and I believe that's true, as after retiring, my wife, our two children, and I relocated to Central Kentucky, where it all started for me.

Life truly is a journey, and we never know the paths or obstacles ahead of us. For whatever reason, the truth is .... I was abandoned, raised in non-familial homes, and at a very young age forced to find my own way. Though I don't dwell on it, questions still remain, such as:

Why did Nettie leave us with a friend rather than family?

If Nettie did try to see us at the Ramey Home, why was she denied access?

Since my birth certificate lists Carl Lake as my birth father, why did Nettie continue to deny that he was my father?

Who gave me the name Roger Ray, and why?

I don't hold resentment as I know things were tough for many in Eastern Kentucky during the 1940s – 1950s. Yet why did it take 40 years for "relatives" to finally come forward, even though Linda and I lived in their community, attending the same churches and school, and were often pictured in local papers?

I guess the real story of my ancestry has been buried along with Ms. Ramey, Nettie Oney, and Carl Lake.

Some people may have used an upbringing such as mine as an excuse to fail – with God's help, I was determined not to let the past define me. During my life, I have tried to find positives and humor in all my endeavors. I believe this attitude and the ever-present encouragement of my greatest asset, my wife Debbie Callahan Ray, who, when I doubted myself, would say, "Why not you?" – you got this! Over our nearly 44 years of marriage, Debbie has made many sacrifices with the belief that God puts us where we need to be. We are forever grateful for the blessings we have received.

We all have choices to make throughout our lives, so my motto has always been "keep the faith, forge ahead". The past is past, live for today and better tomorrows.

www.ingramcontent.com/pod-product-compliance
Lightning Source LLC
LaVergne TN
LVHW021122080426
835513LV00011B/1204